ORGANISATIONS AND INFORMATION TECHNOLOGY
Systems, Power and Job Design

INFORMATION SYSTEMS SERIES

Consulting Editors

D. E. AVISON
BA, MSc, FBCS
*Department of Computer Science and
Applied Mathematics, Aston University,
Birmingham, UK*

G. FITZGERALD
BA, MSc, MBCS
*School of Industrial and Business Studies,
University of Warwick, Coventry, UK*

This is a brand new series of student texts covering a wide variety of topics relating to information systems. It is designed to fulfil the needs of the growing number of courses on, and interest in, computing and information systems which do not focus purely on the technological aspects, but seek to relate these to business or organizational context.

INFORMATION SYSTEMS SERIES

ORGANISATIONS AND INFORMATION TECHNOLOGY
Systems, Power and Job Design

Ian Winfield BA, MA, AFBPsS, C Psychol

OXFORD

BLACKWELL SCIENTIFIC PUBLICATIONS

LONDON EDINBURGH BOSTON

MELBOURNE PARIS BERLIN VIENNA

© Ian Winfield 1991

Blackwell Scientific Publications
Editorial offices:
Osney Mead, Oxford OX2 0EL
25 John Street, London WC1N 2BL
23 Ainslie Place, Edinburgh EH3 6AJ
3 Cambridge Center, Suite 208
    Cambridge, Massachusetts 02142, USA
54 University Street, Carlton
    Victoria 3053, Australia

Other Editorial offices:

Arnette SA
2, rue Casimir-Delavigne
75006 Paris
France

Blackwell Wissenschaft
Meinekestrasse 4
D-1000 Berlin 15
West Germany

Blackwell MZV
Feldgasse 13
A-1238 Wien
Austria

First published 1991

Printed and bound in Great Britain by
Hartnolls, Bodmin, Cornwall

British Library
Cataloguing in Publication Data
Winfield, Ian
Organizations and information
technology.
1. Organizations. Information
systems. Management
I. Title
658.4038

ISBN 0-632-02837-8

Library of Congress
Cataloging in Publication Data
Winfield, Ian.
  Organisations and information
  technology: a practical review/
  Ian Winfield.
    p.   cm.
  Includes bibliographical references
  and index.
  ISBN 0-632-02837-8
  1. Management—Data processing.
  2. Organization—Data processing.
  3. Information technology—
  Management.
  I. Title.
  HD30.2.W56 1990
  658'.05—dc20

DISTRIBUTORS

  Marston Book Services Ltd
  PO Box 87
  Oxford OX2 0DT
  (Orders: Tel: 0865 791155
           Fax: 0865 791927
           Telex: 837515)

USA
  Publishers' Business Services
  PO Box 447
  Brookline Village
  Massachusetts 02147
  (Orders: Tel: (617) 524–7678)

Canada
  Oxford University Press
  70 Wynford Drive
  Don Mills
  Ontario M3C 1J9
  (Orders: Tel: (416) 441–2941)

Australia
  Blackwell Scientific Publications
  (Australia) Pty Ltd
  54 University Street,
  Carlton, Victoria 3053
  (Orders: Tel: (03) 347–0300)

Contents

Series Foreword

The Blackwell Scientific Publications Series on Information Systems is a new series of student texts covering a wide variety of topics relating to information systems. It is designed to fulfil the needs of the growing number of courses on, and interest in, computing and information systems which do not focus purely on the technological aspects, but seek to relate these to business or organisational contexts.

Information systems have been defined as the effective design, delivery, use and impact of information technology in organisations and society. Utilising this fairly wide definition, it is clear that the subject area is somewhat interdisciplinary. Thus the series seeks to integrate technological disciplines with management and other disciplines, for example, psychology and philosophy. It is felt that currently these areas do not have a natural home, they are rarely represented by single departments in polytechnics and universities, and to put such books into a purely computer science or management series restricts potential readership and the benefits that such texts can provide. This series on information systems now provides such a home.

The books are principally student texts but they will also be of interest to practitioners due to their emphasis on practical aspects as well as theoretical. However certain topics are dealt with at a deeper, more research orientated level.

The series is expected to include the following areas, although this is not an exhaustive list: information systems development methodologies, office information systems, management information systems, decision support systems, information modelling and databases, systems theory, human aspects and the human–computer interface, application systems, technology strategy, planning and control, and expert systems, knowledge acquisition and representation.

The latest addition to the Blackwell's Information Systems Series is *Organisations and Information Technology: Systems, Power and Job Design* by Ian Winfield. This book addresses the impact of information technology on organisations and their social environments. Organisations are not simply treated as structures but are recognised to be composed

essentially of human beings. The book takes a wide range of perspectives
and utilises concepts from many disciplines. It clearly reflects the interdisciplinary nature of information systems and is a welcome addition to
the Series. In particular as we believe it is one of the few books to address
information technology from this important perspective and it healthily
balances some of the more mechanistic approaches.

David Avison and Guy Fitzgerald
Information Systems Series Editors

Preface

The title of this book combines two very powerful concepts. On the one hand we have organisations – and organisations, public or private, large or small, rule our lives. Organisations though are increasing users of information technology; and information technology as we all know, has the power to change the world. So what happens then when organisations use information technology? I focus on life in and around organisations: on people's jobs, on their working lives, on the changed shape of organisations, on their politics, their philosophy, what opportunities are open to them and what opportunities are lost forever.

In writing this book I have deliberately used a wide spectrum of sources. I have used established textbooks, research reports, articles, notes and reviews as well as my own experience in human resource consultancy. I have deliberately not dwelt long on the health aspects of working with new technology, nor with industrial relations issues for I feel they have been covered adequately elsewhere. The main issues addressed in each chapter are as follows.

The first chapter is a general introduction to some of the most pressing questions faced by the student when first studying organisations and information technology. It sets out what I hope is a profitable way of classifying types of information technology found in organisations. We examine the general impacts (both positive and negative) the categories of technology have had on employment, people's working lives and gender issues, among others. Research on some new forms of working are also examined: networking, electronic homeworking, autonomous working groups and co-operative software.

Chapter 2 *Implementing business information technology* examines good and bad practice of bringing information technology into organisations. Business organisations successful at implementation can be contrasted with those that are unsuccessful – from this we can draw important lessons for the future. Central to success is knowing just what information technology can do and what it cannot do.

Chapter 3 asks what is information technology actually doing to organisations? Is it changing their shape, their internal power structures, their competitive outlook? The chapter examines the trend towards the integration of functions that technology brings as well as some new emergent shapes of organisations.

Chapter 4 focusses down upon people and their changed jobs within organisations. Information technology has altered the task performance of jobs, but the actual management of the task has not been severely affected. There are strong contrasting forces here: on the one hand we are witness to the emergence of 'electronic sweatshops', mindless VDU monitoring tasks and lousy job design. On the other hand information technology can liberate us forever from the humdrum and boring. We study cases where greater use of skill is allowed and where greater job satisfaction ensues. Some comparisons with European experience are made and the chapter concludes by looking at guidelines for software development and group working using networks.

Chapter 5 looks at management's role in information technology and at the real choices available to it. Studies of good management practice are examined and the total organisational culture is viewed in relation to its technology strategy. It is ultimately management's duty to evaluate the total worth of its investment, and the chapter looks at effective ways of doing this.

Chapter 6 looks at the strategic implications of information technology. The tremendous power that technology gives to the organisation should be matched with a sense of responsibility. The responsible business of tomorrow is socially, politically and ecologically aware.

I wish to record my appreciation to colleagues and students of the Nottingham Business School, Nottingham Polytechnic; to Robin Arnfield, Commissioning Editor at Blackwell Scientific Publications Ltd; but most of all to my wife Elizabeth: her patience and quiet encouragement never go unnoticed.

Ian Winfield

Chapter 1
Types of systems in organisations

1.1 OVERVIEW

Because of the impact of information technology, organisations and their social environments are changing. The kind of change they are undergoing is best understood using not one but many different perspectives; too narrow a focus limits what we can see happening. Different methods of examining the role of information technology in organisations are considered. Information technology found within all business organisations can be classified into five major types, and this chapter concludes by reviewing some of their main impacts. Empirical evidence of the impact of information technology in UK and US organisations is examined.

1.2 INTRODUCTION: ORGANISATIONS AND INFORMATION TECHNOLOGY

When we set out to study organisations and information technology we need to draw on as broad a range of perspectives as possible. Too narrow a focus and we miss essential features. A business organisation, its design, its shape, its working climate and culture, is all due to the history of prior strategic choices. How it uses information technology, indeed *if* it uses information technology at all, is due to human decisions – decisions made about where the organisation is going and how it is going to get there. Information technology is not something grafted on, appendage-like, to an existing organisation. Indeed when it does appear so, it is often mismanaged and doomed to failure. Instead it evolves; it grows out of perceived business and human needs. It is the product of a particular history of human choices; choices it must be said, that are made in a particular social and cultural setting. But to talk about human choice and the cultural effects upon human choice so early in a book examining the effects of information technology on organisations may at first seem strange. Why introduce the 'soft', fuzzy, value-laden concepts of the social sciences in a book about something as cut-and-dried and scientific as information technology? I believe though that the concepts can measurably deepen our understanding of what is happening. For what is happening is taking place in an essentially social context. Knowledge, and indeed information itself, is a social construct.

To the person in the street the very word 'technology' has an imperative ring to it. Associated with the word are phrases such as 'the advance of technology', 'the march of science', 'the relentless advance of research'. All of these have a certain inexorable, determinist flavour. However phrases such as these begin to structure people's thinking about technology. In the popular mind technology assumes a rather chilling guise of something immutable, relentless, somehow inhuman. The naive observer naturally thinks that something similar must happen to organisations once touched by the lifeless hand of technology and that they must be transformed in the same determinist manner. Consequently, reasoning by analogy, if the microchip has transformed aspects of our daily lives then, similarly, organisations and places of work must be transformed as well.

1.3 HOW ARE ORGANISATIONS DESIGNED?
ORGANISATION THEORY REVISITED

But what exactly are the forces behind an organisation which determine its design and the subsequent behaviour of the people within it? Does technology, like an engine, drive the whole organisation? Or does the market determine things? Or might it even be a combination of the two?

A brief examination of the history of organisation theory reveals a steady progression from the belief that there are simple 'laws' that determine the shape and size of organisations, through to the idea that organisations are more complex, more open to the influence of both individual and collective strategic decisions. The history of ways of looking at organisations, including the interpretation of the role of technology as change agent, is beyond the scope of this textbook. Summaries can be found for instance in Perrow (1972, 1973), Winfield (1984) and Handy (1986). In order to examine the impact of information technology on organisations only a relatively few approaches to organisations need to be in our toolkit of ideas. No one perspective standing on its own is however sufficient to explain all that is happening to organisations.

To the student looking for simple truths or for neat, straightforward 'answers' to the myriad problems of organisations and information technology this might seem dismal news. The pure and simple truth, as Oscar Wilde observed, is in reality, rarely pure – and never simple.

For our purposes we shall select just two particular perspectives on organisations and then show how they illustrate features of the problem. The two perspectives have themselves been selected from among what can be construed as the main current dominant perspectives for looking at organisational design and behaviour. (For a review see Van Ven & Joyce 1981.)

Should we despair that there are so many, often sharply contrasting, perspectives on organisation design and behaviour? No, for in the study of organisations this is itself a healthy sign. Organisations, even if we describe them by analogies, say a mechanistic or a biological analogy, remain essentially peopled by human beings. People hold values, and values are passionately argued about. And long may they continue to be argued about too. If values cease to be argued about then we have a sterile, totalitarian society. Any organisation whatever purpose it serves then becomes simply an extension of the state – lifeless, uncritical, unquestioning.

The two contrasting perspectives that will be examined are the 'sociotechnical perspective' and the 'Aston' or 'structuralist school'. These two approaches are ideally suited to explain what is happening to organisations.

1.4 TWO PERSPECTIVES AND THEIR RELEVANCE

The sociotechnical systems approach claims that modern organisations have to be seen as a synthesis between the technical means of production (including information technology) and the social resources of the people who actually constitute that organisation. The two must integrate successfully. This has intuitive appeal for us: implement too advanced a production process and management information system for the work-force to understand and operate, and the system will almost inevitably break down. Preparation, training, consultation, a survey of user needs – all these help 'blend' a technical system with an existing work force.

As exemplified in the work of Jacques (1951), we can best construe an organisation as a multilevel system whose 'layers' affect one another. The so called 'technological imperative' is a legacy from earlier Taylorist thinking: this states that a particular form of production must inevitably lead to a particular form of organisation. The sociotechnical perspective claims however that technological imperatives are not in themselves sacrosanct. Violations of imperatives can often improve rather than undermine actual work productivity. What this means in practice is that in spite of the best, most efficient work study or engineering method, all will be absolutely worthless without due regard to human needs. Sociotechnical systems thinkers force us to deal with the total system (including the workers at all levels) essentially as the system is at present, rather than as we might like it to be. Genuine choice exists also in how to implement production systems – the guiding principle always being that the employees have a right to experience feelings of personal growth and personal enhancement. This was made explicit as early as 1960 by Trist. The goal quite simply was to enhance the dignity and the self worth of man, yet at the same time not to relegate the technical production system to second place. Put simply, profit had to be squared with human values. People, it was argued, work best when given a sense of identity and the opportunity to use their own discretion. Autonomous group working thus became the sociotechnical system byword and self-regulating behaviour the ultimate goal.

From their studies of the introduction of new techniques of coal mining the sociotechnical school could actually advocate firm proposals for designing and setting up new plant. The workforce must be counselled as to their needs: what they perceive as a satisfactory working environment and what they gain satisfaction from. The technology of the production process 'fits' around this. New plants are designed this way now. As we shall see from studies of the implementation of computer systems in offices in chapter 2, the legacy of sociotechnical systems thinking remains strong and lasting. Office automation, a desk-top microcomputer on every office desk, workstations, networking, expert systems – the implementation of all these developments can be seen to be guided still by strong sociotechnical systems thinking. Above all else it is the total work system that has to be considered. The narrow Taylorist approach to the analysis of single jobs is proving fruitless, for it is the primary social workgroup itself that should become central. Efficient work may not be necessarily effective work. How the workgroup regulates itself can be understood best by the science of cybernetics. What command and control structures does the group have, what are the regulators or behaviour, what feedback is used, how is the system tuned to the needs of the organisation? Those are the ideas of the science of control mechanisms applied to groups. Self-regulating systems of internal authority and respect will cater for problems of control. Individuals, it is held, respond well to developing multiple skills and the group itself comes to possess an increased repertoire of skills and abilities. Rather than having their jobs degraded or deskilled, people will pride themselves in utilising a whole new range of skills. As we shall see later in this chapter the impact of computerisation on a wide range of occupations seems to vindicate the sociotechnical perspective.

1.5 SOCIOTECHNICAL SYSTEMS – A RECURRENT THEME

Another feature of the sociotechnical perspective is that job design should be conducted from a standpoint where intrinsic, psychological factors are uppermost. This is not to deny that pay and conditions, the traditional area of industrial relations and trade union concern, are to be neglected. Rather, it is that factors such as opportunity for personal growth and advancement, the challenge of work, the organisation of tasks to give a meaningful texture to the job – all these are to become valued goals. When we examine the relationship of information technology and modern job design in chapter 4, the ghost of sociotechnical thinking is still with us.

People are ends in themselves, and rather than seen simply as extensions of the machine (or 'hired hands') they are to be viewed as resources to be valued and used. 'Joint optimisation' is the phrase used by sociotechnical systems thinkers. 'User involvement' is its modern counterpart, a feature we explore in chapter 2 *Implementing business information technology*. In starting up new plants, sociotechnical practitioners argue strongly for fostering co-operation. Large-scale dialogues are to be prominent features of start-ups, as indeed of any organisational change strategy.

Any organisation undergoing change, whether it be information technology-driven or not, should recognise that it needs to foster healthy debate within (and outside) the boundaries of the institution. Schon (1971) was an advocate of public learning systems within organisations. With the impact of microprocessor-based communication systems within organisations, channels, modes of communication then become of central importance in corporate life. We examine the effects of electronic mail on one organisation undergoing change later in this chapter, and further review organisational change strategies in chapter 5. Management is faced with certain strategic choices in the direction of change. That choice itself should be made from reviewing the widest possible range of options.

1.6 THEORY INTO PRACTICE

Sociotechnical theory claims that a substantial number of current developments in organisation practice are in point of fact derived from its own epistemological base. Whether such an approach represents the

Traditional approach	Sociotechnical concepts
The technological imperative	Joint optimization
People as extensions of machines	People as complementary to machines
People as expendable spare parts	People as a resource to be developed
Maximum task breakdown, simple narrow skills. Taylorism	Optimum task grouping, multiple broad skills. Work enhancement
External controls (supervisors, specialist staff, procedures)	Internal controls, self-regulating systems, autonomous work groups
Tall organisation chart, autocratic style	Flat organisation chart, participative style. Network of workers
Competition, gamesmanship	Collaboration, collegiality
Organisation's purposes only	Members' and society's common good
Alienation	Commitment, involvement
Low risk-taking	Innovation. Risk seeking (within limits)

Fig. 1.1. Current sociotechnical system concepts.

intellectual highjacking of ideas – a form of conceptual imperialism – is a moot point. Nevertheless, the epistemological roots of many of the ideas contained in this book do, in part at least, derive from sociotechnical systems thinking. A list of sociotechnical ideas and the transformations they have undergone when applied to current organisational theory and practice is illustrated in Figure 1.1.

The consultant in organisation development, when first called into an organisation, will be listening closely to how people describe their organisation. The common linguistic universe will inevitably reveal what people think. For example, what is the dominant culture: is cut-throat competition and mindless aggression the order of the day? Though competitiveness may provide the driving force in certain contexts, too often it degenerates into pointless infighting – the situation where more energy is expended fighting rival offices/departments/individuals/sections rather than being channelled to productive ends. The skilled observer, after a relatively short time, is able to place the organisation into either a 'traditional' category or one attempting to build on sociotechnical thinking.

1.7 THE ASTON PERSPECTIVE

Another perspective on organisational design particularly relevant to our task is the Aston or structuralist school (Pugh *et al.* 1975; Hickson & McMillan 1980). The Aston school sets out to test the nature of the relationship between the various elements (explained below) which together constitute an organisation. Since the impact of technology upon an organisation is, as we have noted, both wide and multidimensional such an approach needs our close consideration. To illustrate there are various hypotheses about the relationship between organisational context and structure and subsequent behaviour and work performance. Perhaps the best known direct relationship is between the technology employed and the organisational structure – a relationship first explored by Woodward in 1965. This is discussed and analysed more fully in the following chapter. The primary goal of the Aston school was to attempt to develop scales that accurately measure those aspects of structure and human behaviour that are relevant to organisations. The Aston studies force us to recognise that the major units of analysis are the following: first the organisation departments or major segments of an organisation,

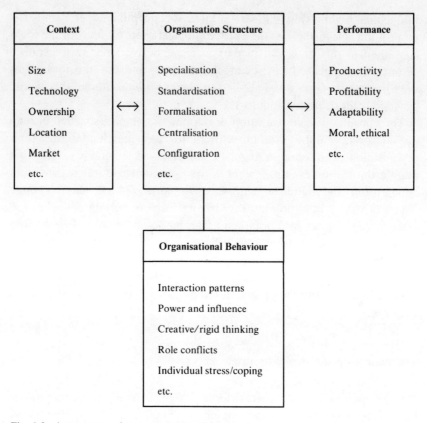

Fig. 1.2. Aston approach to organisational functioning.

second the small groups or teams in offices and, finally, the individual. Figure 1.2 illustrates these relationships.

From the numerous studies conducted by the Aston school perhaps three conclusions merit our consideration. The first is that large organisations that possessed complex but highly integrated production technologies (including CAD/CAM/CBMIS) tended to prescribe in considerable detail the precise nature of people's work activities (technological determinism appears to work strongly here). It was a feature of the Woodward studies that, for example, both the 'one off' production workshop and the small multidisciplinary design studio essentially leave workers to deal directly and flexibly with the client. An informal chat or telephone call as the work progresses is usually all the regulation that is needed. Size and technology appear to alter radically such cosy arrangements.

The second point is that some of the most heavily bureaucratised organisations in the industrial and commercial world are the multinationals. There the degree of formalisation and specialisation of structure is the highest, and it is here in these organisations that economies of scale are important. The best use of labour is achieved by an elaborate, minute division of labour and formal documentation of action is needed for the social control of employees. As size increases the knowledge that one person possesses of the totality of the outfit becomes correspondingly less; the need for the codefication of rules correspondingly becomes more pressing.

In exploring the dimension of bureaucracy the Aston studies found that often 'control press' or the top-down pressure and directiveness associated with a rigid bureaucracy was not nearly as deadening as the received wisdom would have us believe. Surprisingly, bureaucracy in certain circumstances could result in more efficiency and greater job satisfaction than a loose, decentralised structure. This is explored in chapter 4 for studies have been made on the centralising effects of technology.

Of direct relevance to the new generation of 'high tech' entrepreneurs is the Aston finding that successful companies (in terms of growth of sales) operating in variable environments had lower structuring of activity scores than less successful ones. Flexibility and individual autonomy of decision-making appear valuable here. If people are to be alive to new ideas, to product innovation, to the questioning of basic assumptions about any business practice, then repression of any kind has a chilling delaying effect.

1.8 METHODS OF STUDYING ORGANISATIONS AND INFORMATION TECHNOLOGY

Perspectives are useful for helping us fit novel situations and new findings into a framework of understanding. They allow us an historical overview; they allow us to see that computerisation is but another step on the long road of the relentless transformation of society by industrialisation. But how shall we actually proceed to study the transformation of organisations? Is there any one method ready tailored to our particular needs?

To select one particular method to drive our approach would incur the charge of particularism. We might end up searching for evidence to support a chosen method while rejecting other seemingly deviant findings.

1.9 THE SCIENTIFIC PARADIGM

The short answer is that our approach must be scientific. Now this at first seems a sensible answer. Sensible, because the artefact in question, the microprocessor, has itself been developed by nothing short of the scrupulous application of scientific method. It is natural then to assume such an approach would be fitting for the study of microprocessors within organisations.

Organisations and information systems epistemology should, however, be different from the epistemology of pure and applied science. And different in kind. Information systems in organisations, their selection, their use, their shortcomings and their failings, remain solidly within the domain of the social sciences. Information remains information until it is transformed by human effort into something meaningful. Knowledge and information is therefore a social creation. The strict scientific paradigm is of limited use to us in the study of information systems. But let us not throw the baby out with the bath water. The scientific approach is useful to us only in as much as it is useful for studying social behaviour.

The 'strict' scientific approach we shall call positivistic science. This is ideal for the study of microprocessor functioning; it is ideal, too, for basic fundamental research into the underlying physics. Let us look briefly at the basic premises of positivist science so that we can compare it with the requirements needed to study what are essentially social phenomena. Positivist science is characterised by its method of inquiry. Empiricism or trial and error is the main driving force. Everything must have a cause, a cause which is ultimately rationally understood. The universe is a regular system of cause and effect whose regularity needs only to be uncovered and explained by systematic positivist science and inquiry. The scientist then is engaged in what is seen to be a neutral activity; for science, thus construed, is seen as essentially value-free. The product of science is neutral too (though clearly its application need not be!). The foundation of positivist science is indisputably logic and mathematics and thus when phenomena are studied we must attempt to isolate variables; to control for extraneous circumstances, we must measure accurately.

The danger of this approach, admirable and successful though it is for particle physics, is that its premises and methods spill over into the process of studying human behaviour. Indeed a whole school of psychology – behaviourism – was based upon attempts to ascertain universal laws of human behaviour by experimentation in the laboratory environment. Attempting to reduce people to a few sets of fundamental laws or variables to be manipulated is, however, anathema to the best spirit of inquiry about human behaviour. People are not machines, once they are experimented upon in artificial environments they react artificially. Conclusions and 'laws' deduced from such endeavours are limited in real life applicability. Finally the 'detached' observer and recorder of human behaviour is a myth. No one can fail to have expectations, hopes, values about another human being.

Unfortunately the traditional approach to the study of information technology in organisations is heavily coloured by this approach. It is an approach based on engineering. How is this so? Our knowledge of what is happening to organisations should, it is argued, be based on observable, testable hypotheses. The true scientist would argue that we should be able to replicate findings to prove if the theory holds true or not. But do organisations merit study in this way? Can we with any degree of certainty measure and manipulate single variables; can we find out and predict future events? To undertake this we have to do what manifestly we cannot do with people situated in organisations – isolate, manipulate and measure them.

In studying organisations it is people's social worlds, their subjective realities hopes and fears, which are really the object of study, hence the positivist paradigm irretrievably breaks down.

1.10 POSITIVISM IN RELATION TO ORGANISATION STUDIES

Observation, the very cornerstone of empiricism, is never in itself totally value-free, particularly where the observation of human behaviour is concerned. We cannot view people in any system or in any organisation without holding, somewhere within ourselves, some strong positive or negative partisan view. Emotion and feeling lurk beneath the surface. If a researcher engaged in studying any aspect of human behaviour claims to be neutral or dispassionate about his object of study do not believe him. He is covertly supporting the status quo. This covert stance is nowhere better illustrated than in the famous Hawthorne studies. Hailed as the first in-depth analysis of the culture of a factory and using all the panoply of positivist science, it claimed to describe factory life fully, as it was experienced (Roethligsberger & Dickson 1939).

Commentators have however pointed out serious omissions from a study of this purported range and depth (Landsberger 1958). The overall goal of the study was to examine the hypothesis that giving attention to people mattered in organisational life, and the measured improvements in output when attention was given then subsequently proved this true. But the 'objective' study missed a lot. Why for example was there no mention of the process of unionisation in the study of the plant, when it was known to be virulent in the locality and region in which the study was based? Was it simply an omission on the part of the observers or was there something more sinister in the oversight? We can see that the image of the neutral, white-coated recorder of human events begins to break down.

1.11 POST POSITIVISM

Post positivist science regards knowledge not as necessarily true, but postulates instead that what is construed as knowledge is that which is accepted by the community. Even in the fields of 'pure' science we can see that there are dominant, socially-determined fashions for inquiry and theory building. The social construction of science is explained more fully by Kuhn (1970).

Concerning our knowledge about organisations then the so-called 'truths' are true only until a better explanation comes along. Methodological pluralism – obtaining as many perspectives as possible on things – inevitably helps the exploratory theory-testing process along. Organisations should therefore not be viewed as objects to be 'worked upon', as a machine or process which has to be 'intervened', anaesthetised and dissected before it can be understood. This approach can be seen as interventionist: the neutral, dispassionate analyst/researcher as operating upon, dissecting the body politic.

On the other hand, contextualist research recognises that truth, particularly for people within organisations, is in reality multifaceted. The researcher and student of organisational behaviour should be alive to the emergent, holistic features of the organisation. By this is meant that the new paradigm for research should above all else look for life- and value-enhancing features. Information systems which are installed in an organisation to increase its effectiveness should in working life do more than just that. If there is to be any progress in the human condition, we should be actively looking to free people from life-denying work constraints and liberate them from the callous misuse of power.

So often in the past the dominating metaphor of organisational psychology has been that of the mechanism. The approach to studying and researching information technology has essentially been that of engineering. This, in the past, has led to a dominant, essentially simplistic mode of looking at organisations. To think of organisations as if they were machines is to think in terms of something which they are manifestly not. Analogies – mechanistic analogies, organic analogies – all have their heuristic value, but only so far. Often we can be held to ransom in our thinking by being seduced by the metaphor. It can blind us to opportunities, ways of seeing things afresh.

Here are Lyytinen and Klein (1985) on the limitations of information systems design methodologies based on strict engineering principles:

'In the majority of information systems design methodologies, design groups see users as "producers of information" as "primary problem solvers" and as "opponents in an implementation game". Information system development as a process of communicative action through ordinary language is hardly known and rarely studied. In consequence, methods to assist the sharing of different opinions and problems, and the role of ordinary language in this process have not been developed and studied. Because of this most methodologies cannot handle the participation issue or examine it theoretically.'

1.12 STUDYING INFORMATION SYSTEMS: A NEW DIRECTION?

We shall see in chapter 2 the real pitfalls that are to be found when adapting a narrow Taylorist approach to the issue of office automation. In this chapter alternative perspectives are explored in order to avoid the limitations of a narrow engineering approach. It is often said that much of research in organisations and information technology is managerialist, technocist and scientistic. This trio of weighty charges has to be acknowledged. The managerialist charge is made at that broad class of research and writing that is concerned solely with business and organisational efficiency. This research sadly totally ignores the human needs of people working with the information technology in the host organisation. It is the kind of one-dimensional approach that leads to grossly neglected features of job design and people's welfare. These aspects are examined more fully in chapter 4 *Information technology and job design*. The charge of 'technocism' is laid at those writers who firmly believe the 'answer' to problems of work and organisations lies just around the corner. Post industrial society they see is to be a utopia where the 'technological fix' solves all. Much of pop sociology or futurology falls into this category (see for example Toffler 1971, 1980; Bell 1976). For an excellent, if bracing critique of this whole genre see Frankel (1987).

The final charge of scientism we have already examined in relation to the need for an appropriate post positivist stance.

1.13 CATEGORIES OF INFORMATION TECHNOLOGY IN ORGANISATIONS

There exist many systems for classifying information systems technology within organisations. Some, whilst serving useful limited purposes, fall short of the sort of classification we need here. We need a system that is strongly related to the actual impact of technology on the organisation. The impact of an information system on an organisation will be a function of both the system (its design features) and the features of the organisation itself. A classification based on, say, Woodward's type of technology (Woodward 1965) and its various derivatives is inadequate because it is essentially production-based. Post industrial economies are increasingly service-based.

A classification based upon type of user within an organisation is also inadequate because of increasing trends for multi-user systems. The best system, one that is likely to lead to a critical examination of the impact on organisational structure, job satisfaction and people's lives, is a classification based upon system function. We shall adopt a five-fold classification devised by Markus (1984). Many other classification systems exist and there is considerable confusion as to nomenclature to be used. Although labels may be different, the Markus system does seem readily understood by UK readers. This system is illustrated in Figure 1.3.

Operational systems can involve any occupation or hierarchy level

System Types	System Functions	Key Design Features
Operational	To structure work	Work rationalisation Work routinisation
Monitoring and control	To evaluate performance and motivate people	Standards Measures Evaluation Feedback Reward
Planning and decision	To support intellectual processes	Models Data analysis and presentation
Communication	To augment human communication	Communication procedures Communication mediation
Interorganisational	To facilitate interorganisational transactions	Structuring or mediation of interorganisational transactions

Fig. 1.3. Types of system, function and features.

within an organisation. The main focus of operational systems, and the type of work most closely associated with it in people's minds, is to do with the manipulation of material. Examples would be computer aided manufacturing and computer aided materials handling. The focus is clearly on the physical activity of operational systems, though clearly the activity can be primarily intellectual. Bertrand Russell observed that there are two types of work in the world: one type is the manipulation of matter relative to the world's surface; the other type is telling other people how to do it. If the operational activity is primarily intellectual then the system label applied to it falls into our 'planning and decision' category described in figure 1.3. Medical diagnosis systems, strategic planning, operational systems and CAD systems fall into this type.

The key features of operational systems are the need to lower unit labour costs both by work rationalisation and by the attempt to routinise the work itself. The rendering of work processes into a uniform format is one of the guiding principles of Taylorism – a point examined in relation to the implementation of office automation and operational systems in offices in chapter 2. The actual design features of operational systems closely relate to features of the host organisational setting, so that when systems are installed repercussions are felt in job design, job satisfaction and organisational culture. Monitoring and control systems are concerned with analysis of performance: an individual's performance, a department's performance or the performance of total organisational units. The classic example of a monitoring and control system is from the area historically the first to submit itself to computerisation: namely budgeting and standard cost accounting.

Monitoring and control systems are both sophisticated and extensive in function. In today's manufacturing organisation the monitoring and control system can link outputs of machines and individuals and can even integrate information into a total management information system (MIS). Key features of such systems are that precise goals or standards are set; there are actual measures of performance; there is often feedback to the person or persons concerned on performance; and often reward systems (payment) are linked to performance evaluation. Commercial organisations which are at the 'leading edge' in implementing monitoring and control systems often supply examples bordering upon the science fiction.

The Benetton Co system enables the company virtually to sell an article of clothing before it is even made. Many articles are manufactured undyed and then stored. The retail computing system is given a continual update of what colours are selling well and what emergent colour trends and styles are appearing. These data are relayed back to the factory and the stock is then dyed in the colours according to demand. The product design team is kept closely informed of minute fluctuations in the sales. Computer supplied primary sales data closely affect design and production decisions. The J. Sainsbury Co retail system enables the chairman to have on his desk each Monday morning at 8 am a full analysis of the performance of each outlet, and any deviation from the expected sales of each product line. Within each store too, checkout personnel can be performance-monitored and logged. A keystroke counting mechanism allows individual keystroke rates to be monitored. The guiding model of all such systems is the cybernetic model. Cybernetics, or the science of control mechanisms, sees the issue as one of control and regulation. A controlled, regulated system with inbuilt checks and balances, feedback loops and sensing mechanisms allowing for fine tuning is the goal of large-scale systems design in monitoring and control systems.

Planning and decision systems range from humble inventory control to systems designed to generate ideas at the highest corporate levels. The lay person's conception of the floor of the stock exchange or the 'bear pit' of the futures market illustrates the popular idea of such systems. Sophisticated financial models of the market and complex data manipulation are the basic elements of such systems. Developments in the field of decision-support systems allowing human interaction with the system are mentioned in later chapters.

Communications systems sit squarely in the futurologist's domain. As well as the now familiar electronic mail, on the horizon loom voice mail, speech recognition, video conferencing, high definition closed circuit TV and the various satellite-mediated systems. All features of communication systems therefore relate strongly to organisation life, though an especially strong feature is the global scale of today's trade. Today's business reality is geographically dispersed units with trading conducted across global time differences.

An interorganisational system allows transactions between autonomous but independent organisations. For example, the customer can access an airline's booking system via the travel agent. The automatic teller machine allows personal banking transactions without a human intermediary.

1.14 THE IMPACT OF ORGANISATIONAL SYSTEMS

All systems have both positive and negative impacts. Each of the five systems discussed has associated with it a mixture of the two. With systems that are well established and mature we can, due to the extent of research undertaken, reach fairly firm conclusions as to the ultimate nature of the impact, be it positive or negative in its effect on people's working and social lives. With other systems, perhaps undergoing rapid evolution and change, our conclusions may have to be more equivocal. What follows is a brief review of the salient features of the impact of each of the five function systems and a review of some of the key research on such impacts.

As we shall see it seems that each kind of system has with it an underlying dichotomy or series of dichotomies. Sometimes research shows the impact to be in the direction of the popular imagination, while at other times some interesting surprises are in store for us.

1.15 OPERATIONAL SYSTEM IMPACTS

Uppermost in people's minds when operational systems are discussed is the issue of job loss through the computerisation of operations. 'Jobs lost to the computer' was a phrase in common use throughout the UK recession of the early and mid 1980s. It became an issue much discussed in the media, particularly after the media apparently 'discovered' the microprocessor around 1978. Prophets of doom, many of orthodox-left persuasion, heralded the beginning of a workless Dark Age. It was a spectre, they said, that haunted all advanced Western industrial societies. The manufacturing base visibly declined and the sad phenomena of the 'rust belt' appeared. Profound structural changes in employment were taking place as well, for many opportunities were being created in the service industries and in those employment fields directly nurtured by information technology. Travel, leisure retailing and financial services all boomed. The net job loss may in fact have been far less than the doomwatchers predicted (see for example Jenkins & Sherman 1979), so that finally a more balanced picture begins to emerge. As we shall see later in this chapter some major US and UK surveys indicate that when organisations undergo computerisation of operational systems what happens is that essentially a renegotiation of job boundaries take place. There may well be more job changes, retraining and redrawing of job boundaries than actual direct loss of jobs. In the 1990s businesses are starved of personnel with appropriate information technology-related skills that can urgently be transferred to these shortage areas.

The area of discourse concerning operational system impacts has therefore turned much more towards consideration of the opportunities such systems can now offer, and of the opening up of new career prospects and pathways by such systems. To balance this, the critics and cynics (realists they would call themselves) point to the negative effect on job content and job satisfaction. For each avenue of opportunity created, they will cite examples of ever more subtle exploitation by the computer. Production technology, they argue, has in the past often led to intensely alienated workers (Blauner 1964). But does information technology lead simply to either enrichment or to degradation?

Bravermann (1974) first popularised the notion of 'deskilling' in operational systems; he saw the computer removing all human discretion and all skill variety from jobs. What would be left would be mindless button-pressing industrial jobs and armies of regimented mute clones staring intently at VDU screens. The office worker would be a computer-monitored zombie incapable of talking about anything beyond his or her narrow lifeless specialism.

The picture that is emerging is equivocal. In the case of the effects of computer numerically controlled (CNC) machinery and its effect on jobs, Sorge *et al.* (1983) report genuine opportunities for skill enhancement. The authors studied six matched plants in the UK and West Germany. They found that as CNC was applied the forms of organisation and the actual distribution of skills became increasingly varied. Further:

> '... there is no straightforward, unambiguous effect of CNC use on the number of manpower employed. As far as shifts in the composition of skills are concerned the emphasis is less on 'information' skills but on mastering a more demanding cutting process by means of electronic controls which become increasingly easy to use.'

The authors report that far from workers experiencing a loss of control over work processes 'the new CNC technology lends numerical control as never before to total shop floor control'. Participation in CNC programming actually contributes to a spread of skills. Skills may become less polarised and isolated. This is, the authors conclude, directly contrary to the classic finding of Bravermann who, they point out, was researching an earlier form of technology namely numerically controlled machines (wherein tool changes were controlled by digital information). Developments in technology alter the distribution of power and control in the workplace. Only in this case it is in a direction contrary to popular expectation.

The authors point out that the opportunities for contact between operators and programmers and for skill enhancement by operators are unexpectedly high. Programmes are modified and improved during the first runs of production by co-operative contact between both operators and programmers. The authors conclude, somewhat darkly, that what hinders job expansion for operators is the essentially class-based organisation of production within the UK. The UK has much weaker certification of skills in comparison with West Germany, where line hierarchies are much more closely integrated with production engineering functions. In the UK managers are both less well educated and less technically competent than their German counterparts – a point that the UK Government and public opinion seem slow to realise.

'The British type of organisation features a greater amount of lateral segmentation between departments and careers and a numerically strong technical staff superstructure in addition to works personnel. The German organisation, by comparison is distinguished for small technical staff superstructures linked more with supervision and management tasks and investment in technical training.'

Whether the process of CNC results in an increased repertoire of skills thus rests ultimately with cultural and class factors. In the US Skinner (1978) found that potentially positive results from CNC machines were being rendered neutral by a lack of congruence with the factories' infrastructures and employee attitudes, by poor industrial relations climates and training policies (or lack of them). Cross-European trends in the impact of computerisation are as yet difficult to discern. It might be premature to speak of either deskilling or enhancement, for what we have are responses determined in no small part by the history of industrial relations and organisational change. For a comparison of differences in organisation of computer aided manufacturing between France, West Germany and the UK see Maurice *et al.* (1980).

An interesting finding from the UK/West German comparison study was the fact that it was the small plants that were making unconventional use of CNC machinery. They alone appeared to favour a simple, unbureaucratic structure. German companies distinguished less between departments, career mobility was more open and an industrial relations climate actually encouraged polyvalence of skills. In the UK planning, production control and programming remained strictly white collar status.

Larger-sized plants in the UK were often prevented from larger-scale CNC implementation by bureaucratic structures and rigid industrial relations climates, though this point is examined in more detail in chapter 3.

One of the few direct links between organisational structure and computerisation of operational systems lies in the following observation. The greater the horizontal differentiation or complexity of an organisation then the greater the use of computer-based systems. Links such as these trace out the connection between the variables studied by the structuralist perspective.

1.16 ORGANISATIONS OF THE FUTURE?

Operational systems can allow people to work away from a central workplace. People can easily perform data entry tasks or data capture tasks at a workstation in the comfortable confines of their own home. People can program from home; they can access remote databases via necessary telecommunications links; they can call up anything at anytime in any format they wish. Developments in operational systems and remote work are therefore intimately linked with developments in communications systems. Work then can be performed in almost any place, and at any time. First though the often confusing nomenclature surrounding remote work needs to be classified. Remote work is used to refer to organisational work that is performed outside the normal organisational confines of time and space. But remote work can be microprocessor-based or not. The homeworker in garment assembly seated at her sewing machine is as much a remote worker as the home-based systems analyst or self-employed programmer working in the cosy electronic cottage deep in the Surrey countryside. The term 'telecommuting' refers to the capacity of modern communications to replace travelling in to the office. We can see that developments in office automation allow many office workers to be potential telecommuters in that much of their work can indeed be undertaken in their own homes with computer and increasingly cheap communications support (in effect a desktop micro and a telephone line).

Linking remote workers both together and with the central work organisation is referred to as networking. In the UK three well-known examples are Rank Xerox, the ICL network scheme and F International. The basic question posed by organisational designers is this: if people can work and process any amount of information easily from their homes, then why have head offices at all? Rank Xerox has embarked on a large-scale process of employing carefully selected workers on a contract basis. Contracts, that is, involving computer-based work that they can easily do in their own home. Allowing workers to become self-employed on short-term contracts removes the need for the host organisation to maintain expensive overheads such as office space, heating, lighting, building maintenance and such like. (Costs such as these are instead passed on to the contract homeworker.) But whatever the cynics may argue, the actual business results seem superficially impressive. For Rank Xerox the 'experiment', as it was once referred to, has now become a mature established feature of organisational life. It has led directly to 60 new businesses and over 200 new jobs in the few years of its existence (Judkin *et al.* 1985; Coulson-Thomas 1987).

The full history of this scheme and other experiments has yet to be written for just recently anecdotal evidence is tending to temper unbounded corporate euthusiasm. Workers usually cite 'wishing to see more of the family' as the main reason for opting for contract networking. In reality because of the pressures they end up seeing less of the family. Working from home has its own stresses and personnel need to be selected and counselled very carefully. Rank Xerox use sophisticated psychometric tests and personality inventories here. But the main reason people cite when they wish to 'return to the fold' is intense feelings of isolation. They feel isolated from office life; day-to-day gossip; the cut and thrust of normal organisational life. They fear too that they may be left out in the race for promotion and they perceive networking as perhaps some quiet career backwater leading nowhere. A number of critics suggest that networking can lead to a two-tier organisation. There are those decision-makers at the centre (key personnel holding power), whilst round the periphery are scattered easily dispensable contracted workers on short-term contracts with absolutely no decision-making clout whatsoever. This point is developed below.

Before the specific issue of electronic homeworking is examined we have to analyse the opportunities offered to women in software work generally, for the issue of homeworking comes under the topic of females in operation systems. Sexual politics is an issue never far away when considering impacts.

1.17 WOMEN IN SOFTWARE

Programmers can be seen as the prototypical knowledge workers of the future. All sorts of visions and promises abound, some linked to remote office working, some to work in more conventional organisational settings. The reality uncovered by the rapidly growing number of studies of women in software tells a somewhat different story. Kraft (1987) in a survey of 667 software specialists of all kinds found open gender discrimination in wage levels. In 1981 the average US pay for female software workers was $27 400 but for men doing comparable work it was $36 510. Females thus earned on average 85% of the pay of men for comparable work and credentials. Comparable figures exist for the UK; women were to be found in the worst-paying industries that employed programmers – at that point in time it was insurance, finance and estate agency work. The argument for the lag in wages might be that women were not in at the outset of the development of computing and hence they have had little chance to gain the upper echelons of the profession (systems analysts, system managers, project management and so forth). Instead, because of their slow start, they were doomed to be the 'wheel greases', undertaking low level work such as Cobol programming and routine maintenance programming. The researcher claims that women experienced 'blocked careers' with the percentage of women in software remaining the same for the past 20 years (between 20 and 25% of the total software labour force).

In programming then men inhabit the upper regions; women are relegated to the lower regions of the software labour market hierarchy. In this respect computers have merely replicated the traditional relations of the shop floor experienced during all phases of industrialisation: with computerisation there has been no discernible transformation. Two engaging facts however serve to put the nail in the coffin of the 'women not in at the beginning' argument (and disprove the 'women as not possessing the natural aptitude for computing' argument as well). It was a female, 'Ada' or Lady Lovelace, who first helped Babbage programme his analytic and difference engine (the world's first computer) at the beginning of the 19th century. America's first computer, the notorious ENIAC used for the atom bomb Manhattan project at the end of the second world war, was programmed entirely by female labour.

Finally there may be more optimistic events on the horizon for equality of opportunity. The lack of suitably skilled personnel in IT related fields due to the declining numbers of school leavers means that there are more opportunities for women. What feminists have long argued for has been brought about by the economics of supply and demand in the labour market. People seem to be waking up to the gross underuse of talent and to female occupational underachievement. It is now being argued that women, because of generally superior communication and interpersonal skills (listening skills, counselling skills) as well as having higher self-disclosure rates, actually make better knowledge engineers than do their male counterparts (Adam & Bruce 1990).

1.18 WOMEN AND HOMEWORKING

A Department of Employment survey (Hakim 1984) found that one-third of a million women can be classed as homeworkers. One-quarter of a million are married women with dependants. They constitute a hidden, elusive labour force which, whilst in the past used to be engaged mainly in 'out work' (for example small scale assembly or clothing manufacture), is now increasingly found in service work and in non-manual work in clerical and secretarial fields, all of which are becoming increasingly computer-based. British Telecom in their own survey identified 24 occupation groups in total involving more than 13 million people potentially liable to be affected by future developments in electronic homeworking (Upton 1984). The goal of a fibre optic based telephone system will increase the quality of information to be transmitted to and from the home. An upgraded telephone system allied to satellite reception facilities in every home will put the potential homeworker in touch with powerful communication technologies worldwide. Developments such as these can only hasten the trend.

A different, if rather depressing scenario of the organisation of the future is painted by Greve (1987). Because of the dispersal of the labour force brought about by telecommunications she sees a peripheral, marginal group of homeworkers who are easily exploited, doomed to be unable to band together to assert their collective rights and unable to establish decent wages for themselves. The workforce of the future she says can be seen as consisting of two discrete populations. There will be a 'core' group of workers who are highly skilled, well educated, multiskilled and highly adaptable to the organisation's needs. They are on the inner 'fast' track. On the periphery, perhaps loosely connected by short-term or longer-term contracts, will be part-time home-based workers. The largest group of this population will be women. In a study critical of telework or electronic homeworking, Craipeau and Marton (1984) found much of home-based work classified as being undertaken by the 'self-employed' and hence beyond the normal boundaries of employment legislation. They found many grievances, among them a profound sense of alienation among workers, not least because of the electronic mediation of interpersonal relations. They found, too, an undesirable degree of machine monitoring of performance and a poor regard for basic ergonomic considerations in home workstation design. Similar findings relating to the UK are expressed by Huws (1984) and the TUC (1984). Gender-based discrimination is a depressingly common theme of all these findings.

1.19 GENDER-BASED POLARISATION OF SKILLS?

Are organisations that are undergoing the widespread development of computer-based operational systems in all its myriad forms actually fostering gender-based division of labour? An ICFTU study (1983) warns that thinking and planning jobs are being highjacked by males, leaving women to undertake the deskilled, more monotonous repetitive jobs. The report notes that with the advent of computerisation a relatively small number of women workers will find their work upgraded in terms of skill, status and salary; while a large number of jobs which currently need medium skill, discretion and judgement will be replaced by essentially mundane jobs where all the parameters are laid down by the system. Women, it is argued, will find themselves in this occupational dead-end.

A study undertaken in Canada on women service workers (Menzies 1981) found that not one of the female clerical staff affected by computerised operations systems was upgraded or transferred to the newly created and rapidly expanding professional ranks of operations support staff and systems management. This phenonenon was found in the UK by Bjorn-Anderson (1983). What is happening? The argument is that skills and expertise are being transferred to the computer. The ICFTU found that in banking, training time for cashiers had been reduced by 80%. A job which took several years' training (for example data entry) was now undertaken by school leavers able to do the job after a few weeks' training. This points to the fact that in banking methods of intense work rationalisation are being revived, and the current state-of-the art operational systems in banking dictate that work be absolutely standardised and routinised. Jobs in banking are becoming fragmented, there is reduced opportunity for exercising discrimination, and the intellectual satisfaction from seeing the overall broad banking function has decreased. Within banking there has recently been the trend to strengthen behind the scenes IT usage in order to liberate personnel for customer-orientated services. Face-to-face customer contact, advice and counselling are what the customer wants. In personal banking it appears we have a paradox: the higher the level of use of electronics the greater the need for personal contact. The Americans call it the 'high tech, high touch' paradox.

In insurance, too, work has undergone a similar assembly-line transformation as a direct function of computerisation. A Brussels European Community Study concludes 'Office Automation has not enriched job content and has not eliminated repetitive and routine work. Over-rationalisation has resulted in disjointed jobs which offer little support for personal initiative and antonomy' (Lauter 1982). It may be that the advantages first gained in the late 1960s and 1970s in the field of good job design, humanitarian approaches to job design and the Quality of Working Life movement are being eroded by large-scale computerisation projects. In the rush to computerise, sound principles of good job design have been forgotten. This issue is addressed more fully in chapter 4.

1.20 WOMEN, SKILLS AND HOMEWORKING: THE FUTURE?

A more optimistic vista however is painted by Evans (1987) who describes the organisation of F International. Started as Freelance International, it undertakes a broad range of computer-related work: systems analysis, systems management, system design programming, using home-based staff all with home-based workstations. Computer professionals of one kind or another constitute 80% of the staff. Only 8% of F International are office-based. Working from home may, though, involve visits to clients' premises. The founder of the organisation has written enthusiastically of the wealth of talent unleashed by the organisation and the quality of service given to clients by its dominantly female home-based staff (Shirley & Collins 1986). Being tied to the home as a care giver or even being disabled and possessing limited mobility need not deter one from the job market. The telephone line and terminal offers an economic life-line.

But new locations of working brought about by developments in operational and telecommunications systems will inevitably bring mixed responses. There will undoubtedly be opportunities, but there will also be threats: threats in that traditional modes of exploitation will be simply carried over into the new electronic age. Organisations will be denied the traditional methods of supervision and control of workers, so they may well be forced into different, more insidious modes of operation. The work contract will thus be different in kind, a point discussed further in chapter 4.

1.21 MONITORING AND CONTROL SYSTEM IMPACTS

Monitoring and control systems, too, are viewed with caution by many sections of the workforce. Does the advent of sophisticated systems usher in an era of management surveillance of workers, more intense, more terrifying than ever before experienced in nearly two hundred years of industrialisation? Electronic logging of telephone calls, keystroke counting for word processing or retail sales staff, video monitoring, physical movement monitoring, social performance indices – all of these somehow strike at the heart of traditional liberal values. Pre-electronic work entailed scrutiny of human performance based primarily upon the human faculties of eyesight, memory and counting. Just how many visits to the toilet or breaks for a chat or visits to the coffee vending machine or idle moments of daydreaming could the worker get away with? It all depended upon human judgement. Judgement that was fallible. Essentially work rules were open to interpretation and even to social negotiation. An uneven productivity rate in a worker could be tolerated because of local, even personal circumstances. The possibility for intimate surveillance of VDU-based work output has prompted some writers to postulate that there is a qualitative change in the very nature of surveillance.

The pre-electronic worker sold his or her labour; the slave to a VDU sells nothing less than his or her total attention. They are locked into a system which allows absolutely no latitude for attention lapses. Total attention is demanded whether it be supermarket checkout, text or data entry or air traffic control. Fears of surveillance by 'Big Brother', as in the Orwellian nightmare, loom large. Information overload and the possibility of human error, should they be highly consequential, can of course be mitigated by short duty rostas (as in air traffic control). Often though, jobs which are closely monitored by systems seem to fall way short of the principles of good job design. How many people talk of a decline in social interaction, of chance social encounter, of opportunities for genuine convivial interchange in today's electronic office? This theme is returned to in later chapters.

It seems that monitoring and control systems will continue to be discussed in terms of a simple polarity. The polarity of worker freedom versus unnatural, machine constraint. The question of balance has to be resolved through the application of sound principles of job design and sensitive organisational design. Rank Xerox, for example, have succeeded in drastically flattening the organisational pyramid (Coulson-Thomas 1987).

1.22 PLANNING AND DECISION SYSTEM IMPACTS

Like operational systems, planning and decision systems have impacts on job content, on job satisfaction and on job opportunities. The issue of decision-making within the organisation merits our close attention for one over-riding reason: do computer-based decision systems contribute to a change in organisational shape and organisational design? There is no doubt that the availability of vast information-processing power can have profound repercussions on organisational shape. Leavitt and Whisler in 1958 anticipated how the change might affect the future focus of decision-making. Corporate growth in the 1950s and 1960s led to the creation of satellite organisations – offshoots from the centre – in what were dispersed geographical locations. With the continued growth in the economy and sharply rising volumes of business, this inevitably led to information overload back at the controlling centre. The move then became to promote decentralisation: to divest authority and to create semi-autonomous decision-making units. It was the era of the emergence of the regional office, the branch office, the area headquarters. Vast amounts of information flowing from centre to periphery was a management nightmare. With the advent of computerisation and what became in effect virtually unlimited processing power, the head office or headquarters could, it was found, once again handle the mountain of information generated from the periphery. The locus of power and decision-making thus returned, the authors argued, once more to the centre. They argued that decision-making thus will move up, not down the hierarchy. It is a strong argument. Information is power. Processing power is becoming ridiculously cheap. The centre can thus exert a stranglehold on all remote activities if it so wishes.

Actual empirical research on changed organisation shape and location of power within organisations however indicates little or no change. Robey (1981) in his study found that with the implementation of planning and decision systems, original structures became merely reinforced; if change took place at all there was a discernible trend, somewhat surprisingly, towards centralisation. Buchanan and Boddy (1988) in their UK survey likewise found no evidence of large-scale change in organisational power.

1.23 COMMUNICATION SYSTEM IMPACTS

Many of the impacts of communication systems are similar to the impact of dispersed operations systems: a geographically wide network of workers can be established. Current communication system developments are in the field of message systems, teleconferencing, on-line expert systems and voice recognition systems among others. Cheap readily-available communications systems and the growing ease with which information can be transmitted over large distances, often via geostationary satellites, can be said to have contributed to the head office flight from our capitals or large cities. It appears that most cities in the Western world have undergone a degree of change due to high technology manufacture and information technology. Metropolitan economics in particular are being systematically changed by information technology. This impinges directly on urban development and has far-reaching implications for urban planning (for a discussion of the examples of London and Toronto see Hepworth 1987). Office costs, commuting costs, inner-city violence, maintenance and security costs are all being seriously considered when office location is now decided upon. In a sense the luxury of choice is only facilitated by communications technology.

Primary production and distribution units, whether microchip-based or not, are witness to a similar flight. Is the demise of the giant corporation office block just around the corner as this transformation gathers momentum? Giant head office costs are now being looked at more critically then ever before (Dudman 1988). In the past massive investment in head offices may have been protected by steadily increasing property values, but many business analysts argue a slowdown is now imminent.

People are beginning to look critically at total office efficiency. Starting with use. Taking 365 days as 100% the actual utilisation of property is cut immediately to 228 days, or 63% (taking into account the five-day working week, holidays and bank holidays). Offices are only used on average eight hours per day so the theoretical figure of days used drops to 76 or 21% utilisation. Examining the working day, other factors reduce office utilisation still further. Lunch breaks, illness, late arrivals (usually because of traffic conditions) and early leaving bring the operating time down to 57 days or only 16% of the potential.

It is the possibility of computer surveillance of work rate that allows decision-makers to look more critically now than ever before at work output in offices. Simply attending work – selling your time – may have been tolerated in the past; what is now possible and indeed demanded by monitoring and control systems is nothing less than effective work. It is nothing short of people's attention and total dedication to the task in hand which is now being asked for.

Office productivity, as compared with industrial workers' productivity, is low, hence the pressure for the Taylorisation of office work described in chapter 2. At the moment office workers can be seen as dividing their office lives into three parts. First comes the social activity such as organising their own private lives during working hours (telephoning the garage/travel agent/dentist/bank/school/childminder). The next third of their time is spent on running the building or the organisation itself (organising the office party/collecting for leaving presents/charities/ sorting out the office party etc.). Finally the last part of their time can be construed as doing the real relevant work on the proper task in hand (what they are actually paid to do). The office block capital asset is then used a mere 19 days per year or a miniscule 5% of the total available time. It is hard-nosed calculations like these that have led companies such as Rank Xerox to undertake dispersed office working or opt for net-working facilitated by the communications media (Olson 1983).

What effect do changes in communication networks have on the formal distribution of authority? Post industrial utopians see a golden millenium of egalitarian decision-making; an age of new openness of relationships; an age of instantaneous communication with one another in the global village of the modern turned-on, wired-up electronic organisation. This is all good heady stuff but it is an example of totally unreflective optimism. Will communications networks and access by individuals to information in fact break down traditional hierarchical authority patterns? One of the few studies documenting changes that take place with their introduction was undertaken by Emmett in 1981. IBM started their electronic text and message network (Vnet) by installing 400 terminals, connected by a local area network to the central processing unit. The network quickly became a medium for communicating grumbles, soon to become affectionately known among the cognocenti as the 'gripenet'. One bright employee collated all the grumbles relating to the organisation circulating within the network and then mailed them (electronically) to a senior executive. Eruption took place. The employee left, set himself up in consultancy and sold the idea of electronic networking and employee participation to other organisations. He made a fortune. IBM meanwhile, somewhat reluctantly and with a certain amount of embarrassment, had to come to accept and actually encourage the use for which the network was *de facto* being used.

Can systems then be seen to have subversive potential? Studies of early E mail systems (Lippit *et al.* 1980) show they were used primarily for downward communications, a finding endorsed by studies of the Bell system (Leduc 1979) which found increased superior-to-subordination communication. The conclusion seems to be that systems may slightly reinforce but not radically change existing patterns of power within a simple unit or department. If however systems are used across departmental or unit boundaries (as took place in the IBM Vnet example) then the potential for change is clearly much greater. These issues are examined more closely in chapter 3.

1.24 INTERORGANISATIONAL SYSTEM IMPACTS

Interorganisational systems are systems designed to link parties together, often via an intermediary. Electronic fund transfer systems and the common hole-in-the wall banking facility (automatic teller machines) are common everyday examples. UK firms lead the world in the field of paperless trading or electronic data interchange (EDI). It has long been known that major productivity gains can be made by improving intercompany communications. Use of the postal service to move trading documentation physically leads users to refer to surface mail contemptuously as 'snail mail'. The 1990 estimated cost of drawing up and posting an average business document such as a purchase order delivery note or invoice was a stinging £10 an item. EDI works in the following way. A user of components or goods (a retailer or, say, car manufacturer) is electronically linked, via a broker or network, to suppliers. The user can ascertain instantaneously whether there are any stock shortages in the supplier company. It can also see lead times, discount rates and the geographical location of all supplies of the same artefact. It can therefore electronically 'shop around'. Electronic versions of common business documents can then be passed between the computer systems of the two traders, usually via the third party network. By this method British Coal estimates the cost of 35 transactions to be the same as one telephone call (White 1989).

It appears that, initially at least, EDI is growing phenomenally fast with organisations that deal with a large fragmented supplier base. Examples include car manufacture, chemicals, pharmaceuticals, shipping, and the rapid growth in sector-specific networks reflects this (for example 'Cefic', the chemicals industry network and 'Dish' the data interchange for shipping).

Single company systems have been developed largely by the multinationals, such as Ford's Fordnet. Companies are gaining a competitive edge by the use of EDI and it seems likely that the single European market of 1992 will hasten competition and growth in this area. Still further, more and more 'sourcing' is done from overseas (including the Third World) and it has been estimated that at present 7% of the actual cost of goods traded is directly associated with the administrative hassle and delays caused by current pre electronic trade procedures. In hard cash terms this is £50 million of paper log jam (Harkin 1988).

1.25 EMPIRICAL STUDIES OF IMPACTS

In this final section two studies will be analysed: the first was conducted in the UK, the second in the USA. Both are large-scale surveys meriting our close scrutiny for they reveal the extent and nature of the impacts that computer-based information systems have upon organisations and jobs as well as giving us a glimpse of very real cultural differences involved.

The UK study (National Economic Development Office 1983) looked in detail at the effects on 15 companies. Companies studied included

IBM, DEC, STC, British Telecom, Pilkington, Rank Travel and Unipart. Companies were categorised into five general sections: suppliers of information technology, process industries, retailing and distribution, travel and tourism and financial services. Each firm used one or more of our five system types. The objective of the study stated in the preface was a survey 'illustrating a range of situations and ideas rather than providing statistically valid conclusions'.

To begin with the survey found that the role played by external organisations (employer organisations, public agencies and trade unions)

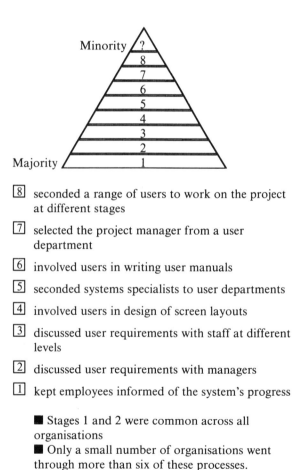

[8] seconded a range of users to work on the project at different stages

[7] selected the project manager from a user department

[6] involved users in writing user manuals

[5] seconded systems specialists to user departments

[4] involved users in design of screen layouts

[3] discussed user requirements with staff at different levels

[2] discussed user requirements with managers

[1] kept employees informed of the system's progress

■ Stages 1 and 2 were common across all organisations
■ Only a small number of organisations went through more than six of these processes.

Fig. 1.4. Employee involvement in implementation (from National Economic Development Office 1983).

was minimal. What did emerge however was a wide range of approaches to employee involvement in implementation. Most organisations kept users dutifully informed, while only relatively few undertook direct formal contact with end-user representatives. In between lay a range of options, illustrated in Figure 1.4.

When the survey came to examine employment effects, the least frequently encountered event was actual job elimination. More frequently tasks became transferred, for example one job became swallowed up by another, as happened in word processing. 'In all, about half of all the case studies showed work being transferred away from dedicated text production or data entry staff to others who added information entry to their job as a subsidiary activity.' Job enlargement and the possibility of job enrichment (making the job more psychologically satisfying) became prevalent.

Many jobs took on new responsibilities; for example secretaries added, among other activities, co-ordination roles and information retrieval from large databases. 'The majority of case studies contained examples of this kind, frequently based on the loss of routine "paper chasing" work which led to greater emphasis being placed on the use of initiative and foresight.' Job losses were difficult to ascertain accurately simply due to the problem, so often encountered, of establishing a genuine baseline measure. Organisations are rarely in a steady-state when it comes to their labour requirements. Few of the organisations could point to definite 'before and after computerisation' time frames in order to measure the effects accurately. Of the 15 companies studied two reported no change in employment level, three said computerisation definitely inhibited growth in employment and one claimed computerisation had directly contributed to a three-fold growth in employment over four years. Nine companies reported a reduction in staff levels. Types of job lost were: data preparation operatives, clerk typists, machine operators, transport clerks and repair service clerks.

The majority of jobs created were technical jobs concerned essentially with data processing and management services: jobs such as knowledge engineers, computer management specialists and other computer specialist jobs. Another class of jobs created comprised those specifically to do with interpreting and exploiting the wealth of management information created by the systems themselves. Finally, training posts in computing-related areas were created. All were at graduate level, thus adding weight to the polarisation of skills argument mentioned earlier.

Specific issues of job boundaries and the changing nature of work for various occupations will be returned to in chapter 4. The overall impact for the remaining jobs was much greater satisfaction, for the jobs that remained required greater use of discretion, initiative, understanding and creativity. A general observation was made on the raising of the level of skill demanded and the broadening of the jobs. Management were required to become technically literate (or 'computerate') for they found themselves much more deeply involved in systems design than ever before.

This generally optimistic note was similarly sounded by a study undertaken in the USA (Kling 1978). The survey covered 1200 managers,· data analysts, accountants and urban planners in 42 municipal government agencies. Most were beginning to use computer-based reports and they reported direct job expansion as one noticeable result. Subjects surveyed also felt an increase in job pressure due to computerisation, but not of closeness of supervision. (Monitoring systems were not in widespread use in the late 1970s.) Computer use, they concluded, had a perceptible, but not dominant effect on their jobs. Over 40% attributed increases in skill, variety and feedback from the job itself directly to increased computer use. Over 30% attributed increases in feelings of task significance and in satisfaction with dealing with others directly due to computerisation. Occupational differences were noted in the same direction as that of the UK. Managers experienced greater benefits to their jobs from system use than did clerks and persons lower down the occupational hierarchy.

1.26 CONCLUSION

This first chapter has examined some of the most useful ways of looking at organisations if we are concerned about the effects of information technology. It is helpful to see an organisation as a delicate mesh between a social system and its technical system. The effect of change in any one system will therefore be felt throughout the other.

Since organisations are populated by humans we need ways of studying their behaviour that are ecologically valid. People's experiences, wants and wishes are just as important areas of scrutiny as are output, absenteeism and bottom-line profitability.

The chapter has used but one among many systems of classifying the types of information technology in use. We see here that all types of system seem to bring both opportunities and threats. Finally, from empirical studies of impacts, we can see that the computer is not always leading us to doom and gloom where jobs are concerned. Findings are emerging which point to increased satisfactions and pride in work. Computer use yields an enriched working life. However, complacency in just assuming that human values are automatically being injected into work by computer use is uncalled for. Extreme vigilance is required, no more so than in the thorny area of the implementation of systems in organisations. This we examine in the next chapter.

1.27 REFERENCES

Adam A. & Bruce A. (1990) Do women make better knowledge engineers? *Computing*, 8 February.

Bell D. (1976) *The Coming of Post Industrial Society*. Penguin Books, London.

Bjorn-Anderson W. (1983) The changing role of secretaries and clerks. In *New Office Technology: Human and Organisational Aspects* (Ed. by H.J. Otway & M. Peltu). Francis Pinter, London.

Blauner R. (1964) *Alienation and Freedom*. University of Chicago Press, Chicago.

Bravermann H. (1974) *Labour and Monopoly Capitalism*. New York Monthly Review Press, New York.

Buchanan D. & Boddy D. (1988) *Organisations in the Computer Age*. Gower, Farnborough.

Coulson-Thomas C.J. (1987) The Rank Xerox networking programme, *Information Technology and Public Policy* 5, 93, 200–204.

Craipeau S. & Marton J.C. (Eds) (1984) *Telework: the Impact on Living and Working Conditions*. European Foundation for the Improvement of Living and Working Conditions, Shankill Co. Dublin.

Dudman J. (1988) In the temples of inefficiency. *Daily Telegraph*, 23 February.

Emmett R. (1981) VNET or Gripnet. *Datamation*, November, 48–58.

Evans P. (1987) Women homeworkers and information technology – the international experience. In *Women and Information Technology* (Ed. by M.J. Davidson & C.L. Cooper). Wiley, London.

Frankel B. (1987) *The Post Industrial Utopians*. Polity, London.

Greve R. (1987) Women and information technology: a European perspective. In *Women and Information Technology* (Ed. by M.J. Davidson & C.L. Cooper). Wiley, London.

Hakim C. (1984) Homework and outwork. National estimates for two surveys. *Employment Gazette*, January, 7–12.

Handy C.B.H. (1986) *Understanding Organisations*. Penguin Books, Harmondsworth.

Harkin F. (1988) Ending the paper chase. *Computer Systems Europe*, December, 34–5.

Hepworth M.E. (1987) The information city. *Cities*, August **4**(3), 252–62.

Hickson D.J. & McMillan C.J. (1980) *Organisations and Nature: the International Aston programme*. Saxon House, Farnborough.

Hirschheim R. (1985) Information systems epistemology: an historical perspective. In *Research Methods in Information Systems* (Ed. by E. Mumford, R. Hirschheim, G. Fitzgerald & A.T. Wood-Harper). North Holland, Amsterdam.

Huws V. (1984) *The New Homeworkers*, Low Pay Unit, London.

ICFTU (1983) *New Technology and Women's Employment Report to the Women's Committee*. International Confederation of Free Trade Unions, Geneva.

Jacques E. (1951) *The Changing Culture of a Factory*. Tavistock, London.

Jenkins C. & Sherman B. (1979) *The Collapse of Work*. Methuen, London.

Judkin D., West D. & Drew D. (1985) *Networking in Organisations: the Rank Xerox Experiment*. Gower, Farnborough.

Kling R. (1978) *The Impact of Computers on the Work of Managers, Data Analysts and Clerks*. Public Policy Research Organisation, University of California, Irvine.

Kraft P. (1987) Computers and the automation of work. In *Technology and the Transformation of White Collar Work* (Ed. by R.E. Kraut). Lawrence Erlbaum, New York.

Kuhn T.S. (1970) *The Structure of Scientific Revolutions*. University of Chicago Press, Chicago.

Landsberger H.A. (1958) *Hawthorne Revisited: 'Management and Worker' its Critics and Development in Human Relations in Industry*. Cornell University Press, New York.

Lauter J. (1982) *L'Egalité des Chances dans le Secteur Bancair dans les Pays de la EEC*. European Community, Brussels.

Leavitt H.J. & Whisler T.C. (1958) Management in the 1980s. *Harvard Business Review*, Jan–Feb, 127–36.

Leduc H.F. (1979) Communicating through computers. *Telecommunications Policy*, 235–44.

Lippitt M.E., Miller J.P. & Halamaj J. (1980) Patterns of use and correlates of adoption of an E Mail system. *Proceedings of the American Institute of Science*, Las Vegas, November.

Lyytinen K.J. & Klein H.K. (1985) The critical theory of Jurgen Habermas as a basis for a theory of information systems. In *Research Methods in Information Systems* (Ed. by E. Mumford, R. Hirschheim, G. Fitzgerald & A.T. Wood-Harper). North Holland, Amsterdam.

Markus M.L. (1984) *Systems in Organisations*. Pitman, London.

Maurice M., Sorge A. & Warner M. (1980) Societal differences in organising manufacturing units: a comparison of France, West Germany, and Great Britain. *Organisational Studies*, **1**, 59–86.

Menzies H. (1981) *Women and the Chip: Case studies of the effects of Informatics on Employment in Canada.* The Institute for Research on Public Policy, Montreal.

National Economic Development Office (1983) *The Impact of Advanced Information Systems.* National Economic Development Office, London.

Olson M.H. (1983) Remote office working: changing patterns in space and time. *Communications of the Association for Computing Machinery,* **26**(3), 182–7.

Perrow C. (1972) *Complex Organisations: A Critical Essay.* Scot, Foresman and Co, Glenville, Illinois.

Perrow C. (1973) The short and glorious history of organisations theory. *Organisational Dynamics,* Summer.

Pugh D.S., Mansfield R. & Warner M. (1975) *Research in Organisational Behaviour: a British Survey.* Heinemann, London.

Robey D. (1981) Computer information systems and organisational structure. *Communications of the Association for Computing Machinery,* **24**(10), 679–87.

Roethligsberger F.J. and Dickson W.J. (1939) *Management and the Worker.* Harvard University Press, Cambridge, Mass.

Schon D.A. (1971) *Beyond the Stable State: Public and Private Learning in a Changing Society.* Temple Smith, London.

Shirley V.S. and Collins E. (1986) A company without offices. *Harvard Business Review,* Jan–Feb, 127–36.

Skinner W. (1978) *Manufacturing in the Corporate Strategy.* Wiley, New York.

Sorge A., Hartman G., Warner M. & Nicholas I. (1983) *Microelectronics and Manpower in Manufacturing: Applications of Computer Numerical Control in Great Britain and West Germany.* Gower Press, Aldershot.

Toffler A. (1971) *Future Shock.* Pan, London.

Toffler A. (1980) *The Third Wave.* Collins, London.

Trist E.C. (1960) *Socio-Technical Systems.* Tavistock, London.

TUC (1984) *Women and Technology.* TUC, London.

Upton R. (1984) The 'home office' and the new homeworkers. *Personnel Management,* September, 39–43.

Van Ven A.H. and Joyce W.R. (1981) *Perspectives on Organisation Design and Behaviour.* Wiley, New York.

White K. (1989) UK widens the EDI net. *Industrial Computing,* March, 19–20.

Winfield I.J. (1984) *People in Business.* Heinemann, London.

Woodward J. (1965) *Industrial Organisation.* Oxford University Press, Oxford.

Chapter 2
Implementing business information technology

2.1 OVERVIEW

This chapter reviews the problems associated with the implementation of information technology in organisations. Studies show that poor success with implementation often stems from inadequate analysis of what organisational needs really are. Using the example of what has occurred with office automation we examine how an approach drawing on multiple perspectives might more accurately describe actual office activities and hence genuine user needs. This approach will be useful in the next wave of implementation of information technology in offices of the future. Various management approaches to implementation are described and evaluated and two models of planning and design are discussed and analysed. The chapter continues by evaluating published implementation guidelines. These guidelines have been drawn up from the study of both successful and unsuccessful companies engaged in implementation. The chapter continues by examining emergent trends in user needs and the need for careful evaluation of information technology, and concludes by examining resistance to implementation.

2.2 INTRODUCTION

'There is nothing more difficult to take in hand, more perilous to conduct, or more uncertain in its success than to take the lead in the introduction of a new order of things'

Niccolo Machiavelli 1469–1527

Niccolo Machiavelli was a Florentine statesman and writer. He is perhaps best known for his approach to politics and human relationships, advocating as he did an amoral approach completely destitute of regards for feeling and consequences. For Machiavelli expediency rules. Today his name is usually uttered with a shudder for he is accused, among other things, of providing the theoretical underpinnings of totalitarianism and the martial spirit. If, within the world of business, you are unfortunate enough to become labelled as a 'Machiavellian type' you know that you are seen by others (your enemies) as being crafty, cunning, manipulative and totally devoid of scruples. Do not despair though, for they may be qualities essential for survival in certain organisational cultures. They may even help you implement new technology in certain types of organisation.

Although Machiavelli's name today has a pejorative ring to it, let us not forget that nevertheless he was a shrewd observer of human nature. As our opening quote shows, even though he was born long before industrialisation transformed the world, he was more than sufficiently versed in the ways of the world to know one fundamental truth about the human condition: despite what people may say about change, basically they hate it. It is as true today as it was five hundred years ago.

People hate change because humans, like all the higher mammals, are essentially creatures of habit. The easy way is to follow established routines, follow well-trodden paths, minimize mental effort by slavishly following time-honoured established practices. If change is in the direction of our own self-interest, say in gaining more profit, then of course we will change. Therein lies the essentially speculative nature of business, the very engine of transformation of the world that businesses big and small bring about. But note, though, that the carrot here is only the attraction of the ultimate ease with which we can do in the future by changed practices what we are doing by sweated labour now. The problems surrounding the implementation of information technology in organisations thus immediately bring us up against a whole range of primitive human fears and desires. Often they are half realised, half submerged fears and desires that are so deep as to be barely faced squarely during waking hours. How many employees or businessmen have lain awake in the small hours and asked: 'Am I getting old fashioned, am I missing out on new ways of doing things?' 'Am I really up to learning this new system?' 'Am I falling behind the times?' When we talk of primitive fears and desires, of wants and needs, we are on territory which is familiar stamping-ground of advertising and persuasion techniques. These, as we shall see, have had – and still have – an important part to play in the implementation game.

2.3 PRODUCT PUSH

Information technology is driven by new product ideas, by customer demands, competition and business needs. Change results from the steady flow of products purporting to do things faster and better than ever before. As we all know the businessman is continually pressed to invest in the latest fashion, to keep ahead of the competition by possessing the latest new-fangled innovation. The vendor then becomes an important element in understanding implementation decisions. The vendor sells the product: the product itself then assumes the status of cult object – a phenomenon accurately labelled by Karl Marx as the 'fetishism of the product'. The product comes to assume the role of universal panacea. The need to rush into purchase of the (usually) latest 'labour-saving' gadget often is fuelled by manipulative advertising hype. Make no mistake: it is hype carefully engineered to play upon people's sense of inferiority. Of the millions of desktop microcomputers sold to the market segment identified as 'the small businessman', but a fraction are up and running after one year; smaller still is the number of systems that have genuinely earned their capital outlay, let alone contributed to the much promised increased revenue and profit.

However, standing opposed to the barrage of advertising hype are a growing number of non-partisan, balanced guides advising the potential purchaser first and foremost if a system is needed, how to choose systems, what to look for, how to implement them and how to evaluate them. (See for example Aziz 1986; Clegg *et al.* 1988.) As we shall see later in the chapter, there is a growing body of research literature critically examining the drive to implement computers indiscriminately, and in particular the drive to automate the business office. Vendors stand accused of overselling short-term capabilities and relegating crucial human issues to the sidelines. The issue of vendors and fraudulent misrepresentation of capabilities has been well documented by Markus (1984). Case studies of litigation battles against 'big name' manufacturers and suppliers make engaging reading in the appropriate journals and quality press.

The cultural focus of much of the implementation of the 1970s and early 1980s was on installing the answer, finding the quick solution, finding the quick 'technological fix'. The focus was on the technical capabilities of the machine and its promise – an approach we shall term 'technocentrism'.

2.4 SHORTFALLS

Many studies have been made of the shortfall between the promised utopia that business information technology offers and the actual dismal business reality, be the organisation large or small. These reports make sobering reading. The work of Damoderam (1986) is typical of such studies. After a large national bank installed an expensive desktop system the researchers found that many facilities were rarely or never used by staff. Four out of a possible 33 facilities accounted for 75% of use. Half of the facilities provided remained unused after one year! In a survey of the design and implementation of computer-based management information systems in small companies Wroe (1985) found that of ten companies setting out to implement systems only four proceeded to successful implementation.

Blackler and Brown (1986) conclude their survey of implementation practices in the UK with the following observation:

> 'The research indicated that the standard of planning of the introduction of new technologies is often poor with, for example, applications of the technology often being poorly integrated into broader business objectives and, beyond a very limited concern with ergonomic considerations, organisational and psychological issues remain unrecognized.'

The conclusion from the studies of the implementation of large-scale systems (across all functional types) in large organisations is basically the same conclusion we obtain from studies of small business experience with the 'low cost' microcomputer. Needs are inadequately analysed, goals are poorly specified, systems are often ill-chosen and people are ill-prepared for change. Organisations may have been sold apparatus not squarely in line with their critical needs; 'product push' and 'product oversell' on the part of suppliers may have simply gone too far. What we need to do is concentrate on an accurate definition and analysis of what the system actually is that we intend to upgrade or replace. Although computer-based systems in organisations can be classified into one or more of the five function types outlined in chapter 1, all, save a few exceptions, are actually implemented into what can be termed as office environments. The central office or decision-making hub still seems to be an enduring feature of organisation life, despite innovations in contracting out, networking or remote electronic office working. Correct analysis of office needs can thus serve as a useful paradigm.

Our analysis covers monitoring and control systems installed in offices, computer-based management information systems, financial information systems and the technology associated with communications systems. We include as well the first drive to automate the office: the humble desktop micro and applications such as the software of word processor, spreadsheet and database. What does the research into the recent history of computer-based office automation yield to make this area such a useful textbook example? In 1982 the UK Government undertook a pilot scheme to promote office automation. Its stated goal was to broaden user experiences with office automation and it gave funding of up to £250 000 per pilot project. (Significantly to qualify, each project had to incorporate a technological 'innovation' – a case of the seduction of the new gadget?) The report after four years of the project (Pyre *et al.* 1986) found that only a few of the 20 pilot schemes were successful. Once again, the business reality fails to match the glittering promises.

2.5 WHY AUTOMATE AN OFFICE?

Office worker productivity is low in comparison to that of the industrial worker. The impacts of Taylorism, of work study, of organisation and methods techniques have radically helped efficiency on the shopfloor; less so in white-collar office work. Poppel (1982) suggests that office costs may account for up to half of total corporate costs, and while industrial productivity may have risen 90% in the past decade office productivity has risen a mere 4%. From this we can see that the desire to automate is enormously strong. The office, in order to become more efficient, should be construed as nothing short of an assembly line. Office automation in the form of computer-based office technology can be seen as the modern Trojan horse of Taylorism. We wheel it into the office naively hoping to revolutionise productivity and jack up profits.

2.6 ANALYSING OFFICE FUNCTIONING: THE OFFICE ACTIVITIES APPROACH

Information technology is brought by organisations into the office purportedly to support the user and to save on escalating office costs. That so much hardware so often remains underused or fails in some way to reach its full organisational potential shows that both user and organisational needs have failed to be adequately analysed. 'Offices' vary enormously and are, relative to shopfloor work, engaged in essentially loosely structured or even unstructured work. The first pressing need then is to analyse and label adequately what people actually do in their offices. A common approach has been to take what is termed a Taylorist task-orientated approach (Taylor 1911). This is simple. A stopwatch is taken to office personnel and a rough and ready breakdown of their working day is undertaken. This is termed the 'office activities' approach. Hirschheim (1986) cites studies of office principles (management and professional staff) showing the following breakdown of time spent in a typical working day:

	%
Meetings	12
Writing	15
Telephoning	12
Reading	7
Calculations	6
Travelling	6
Filing and retrieval	5

Secretarial and typing staff had the following:

	%
Typing	37
Telephoning	10
Mail	8
Filing and retrieval	7
Copying	6

Using a somewhat different technique, Blackler and Brown (1987) found UK managers undertaking the following:

	%
Talking	27
Paperwork	44
Calculating, planning and travelling	29

A study by Bair (1987) of 250 000 'knowledge workers' in US corporations and government departments gives:

	%
Face to face	32
Written communication	20
Telephone	13
Other activities	35

Despite manifest variations between studies due to different measurement techniques and classifications, all of them seem to point to a high incidence of face-to-face, interpersonal communication. This seems particularly so for managers and professionals. Face-to-face contact is essential for activities such as negotiating and counselling, bargaining and selling. Human support is needed too when investigating the reasons behind a decision or when trying to assemble staff for a meeting. Using a strictly Taylorist interpretation it could be said that office staff spend a sizeable portion of their time in what can be construed as relatively unproductive ways. It seems a good idea then to let information technology do the donkey work or the 'mental navvying' by, say, holding and transferring telephone calls, by cutting down travelling time, by undertaking video conferencing and so on. This may be true for these specific social functions, but the main thrust of the 1970s, 1980s and early 1990s office automation was in designs which ignored the important social aspects of office work – and particularly so for managers. It assumed that all office work was to do with spreadsheets, database manipulation and specific applications packages such as word processing.

When office workers are asked about their wants, they are inevitably disposed towards citing what is currently popular and what is selling well, and so manufacturers and designers for their part will supply products that unfortunately only partially solve the problem. Damoderam (1986) claims that the design of office automation products and systems ignores the human contact and human interactive element, or presupposes them to be at an absolute minimum. Manufacturers presuppose office work is number crunching and quantitive decision-making. In the first wave of word processing aimed at reducing secretarial and typing costs, manufacturers may have got it right: the typist spent less time on costly revisions of office documents, and typist and secretarial costs were correspondingly dramatically reduced. Strassman (1985) notes that secretarial costs rise because more copies are done and more time is spent redoing work because it is easier to do. The 1980s and current 1990s wave of office automation is this time targeted at managers and office principals. It still carries on in the same essentially Taylorist vein, however their work is different in kind. Here is Damoderam on the work of office principals:

> 'Such interactive tasks cannot be performed by available office technology although the technology can assist them. These tasks and a number of similar activities have been identified as the 'hidden work' generally conducted by support staff such as secretaries in the office situation. Replacing such staff with devices designed to facilitate more rapid generation of text etc. clearly leaves the executive to carry out the previously 'hidden work' himself. It is easy to see that in such circumstances efficiency of the total office system may well fall short of the predicted gains.'

Here lies the heart of the problem. Managers may be loath to take onboard computer-based office technology because they recognise an extra workload attached to it. In exactly the same way many managers (usually male) resisted the microcomputer because the keyboard was associated with typewriter work – essentially 'infra dig'. The error stems from the fact that we are not, in the first place, measuring or describing the correct genuine nature of office work for office principals. Our measurements and prediction of needs may be wrong because we are using the wrong tools. It is an interesting approach to the analysis of shortfalls and is in itself worthy of further consideration. More so when we look into the emergent office needs of the 1990s.

2.7 UNDERSTANDING OFFICE WORK: ALTERNATIVE PERSPECTIVES

The task-orientated office activities approach to the understanding of future automation needs is essentially Taylorist in conception. This means in practice that goals are supposed to be clearly known. A time-and-motion approach seems satisfactory. Simple, goal-directed work (the production or setting of goals) can be broken down into its constituent parts merely by observation. The surface or publicly recordable activities that people perform during work are what count most. This activities approach is what has driven the manufacturer and implementer of office technology alike.

An alternative, diametrically opposed approach would be to analyse not the superficial features of office work, but the subjective meaning it

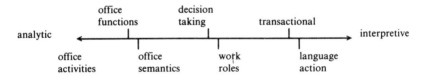

Fig. 2.1. Perspectives and views of the office (after Hirschheim 1986).

has for the participants. This approach sees work in offices as socially orientated. The social aspect of work is here not regarded as a side issue, rather it is regarded as central to people's office lives – particularly so for office staff who are decision-takers. Between the two extremes of the analytical or task-orientated approach and the interpretive or socially-orientated approach lie many alternative perspectives for viewing the office. All of them have something to contribute to our understanding of the reality of office life as it is daily experienced. These are illustrated in Figure 2.1.

A consideration of alternative ways to describe office work will allow a richer, more varied description of what is going on; for office behaviour is, in case we forget, primarily social behaviour. Social behaviour is multifaceted and open to different interpretations according to viewpoint and level of analysis. Office work is a rich mosaic of behaviours – behaviours coloured by people's wants and desires – so to describe and understand it we therefore need tools and concepts considerably more sophisticated than the crude mechanical stopwatch. But our many viewpoints and approaches should be construed not as mutually exclusive, but as basically complementary to one another.

In figure 2.1, moving from the analytic Taylorist extreme we can see office personnel as performing certain functions. Office functions are structured by listing the roles, the tasks and the expectations of behaviour and, of course, perhaps duties and responsibilities. Thus office proce-dures are sequences of events that some physical object progresses through to reach its goal. The progress of a claim through an insurance office is an example of an office function.

An 'office semantics' view tries to understand why people perform the activities that they do. All information-processing acts are necessarily driven by intention, conscious or otherwise. Thus the finance director scans the summary budget statement looking for deviations from the expected figures. If asked, he will say that he is driven by the need to explain the differences between the observed and the expected.

Offices, though, are areas where decisions are made. The consequences of a particular decision for the organisation can in certain cases be monumental in outcome and bear no relation to the actual time spent reaching that decision. The 'timed activities' approach to analysis of activities may be less than useless here. Specific applications software, expert systems and decision-support systems are targeted at this specific interpretation of office activities.

To see the office as an arena for acting out role demands has been admirably documented by Mintzberg (1973). The manager, for instance, has three main roles: interpersonal, information-processing and decision-making. The various interpersonal roles he or she may have include being a figurehead or leader; whilst the information role includes monitoring and/or disseminating information, editing information or being a spokesperson. In the decision role the manager is variously entrepreneur, intrapreneur, disturbance handler, allocator of resources or negotiator between parties.

The transactional view of the office brings us much nearer to the socially-negotiated end of the spectrum of interpretations. Here the office is seen as an arena for information exchange based upon contracts. Contracts are continually being negotiated and modified, for the social world as we experience it is in a constant state of flux. For example, power struggles are a daily feature of organisational life and are ignored at one's peril. Individuals behave opportunistically; individuals behave irrationally. Likewise the office can be seen as an arena for the battle between the sexes. Women, collectively and individually, so often feel precluded from the upper echelons of the organisation; they feel strongly that they are denied their rightful power. The office may therefore be seen as a battleground to assert rights, to make demands, to apply pressure.

The remote electronic office located in the home supplies many examples of this type of socially-negotiated order. First an area in the family home has to be designated either exclusively or part-time as an 'office'. What are lawful and unlawful intrusions into the privacy within the designated 'office' have to be worked out. If it is said that the workshop, garage or shed is the last bastion of uninterrupted male introspection (Greer 1984) what sort of social and spatial reality does the harassed male office worker attempt to create at home? What is the reality for female homeworkers?

People choose remote office working – away from the central organisation – ostensibly to see more of the family, but report actually seeing less of the family when working in the home. What then are the elaborate sexual divisions of labour that must ensue from implementation of electronic homeworking? Changed family circumstances and changed patterns of interaction can only be satisfactorily interpreted by a transactional approach, an approach that sees it as a fluid, emergent social system complete with subtle checks and balances.

As a final approach one could enter an office and simply study the speech of the occupants. What might this reveal? It would reveal informal, non goal-directed speech acts, for obviously people go to work for social reasons as well as for financial. The reasons people cite for resisting a change to homeworking or in returning from homeworking into the organisational fold are that they miss the social cut-and-thrust and do not want to miss out on the promotion stakes. The 'language action' approach is based on the work of Habermas (1980). Language in an office is used mainly for technical control, for clarification purposes, for improving communication or for attempting to free us all from constraints upon our freedom. We thus say that discourse in an office is 'rational' if it is both critical and informed talk. Agreement in an office can of course be illegitimate (let us say if it is an imposed agreement). Agreement to be legitimate must, says, Habermas, be grounded on valid and true knowledge. An office system should then be subject to the social, collective approval of all concerned. For undistorted information to be exchanged the speech acts of all concerned must be intelligent, truthful, adequate and accurate. In reality, as we all know, there are many barriers to communication. There may be bias on the part of the sender or receiver of the message; information becomes channelled for reasons of power; coded meanings can be exchanged and a nod or a raised eyebrow totally reverses the meaning of a message.

To conclude, the office as an arena for change is best analysed using as many valid perspectives as possible. Only then will the richness of genuine social experience at work be fully documented. Failures or shortcomings in organisational implementation of computer-based office automation can only be satisfactorily explained by drawing on these multiple perspectives.

2.8 IMPLEMENTATION STRATEGIES AND TECHNOLOGICAL DETERMINISM

The complexities and subtleties of office behaviour described at the social end of the spectrum may be close to the subjectively-experienced social reality of office workers. But the Taylorist mode of interpretation is what in the past guided manufacturers and dictated implementation strategies. Implementation was based solely on cost-saving criteria, and during the 1970s and 1980s it was the service sector which felt the worst pinch of labour-saving devices. Implementation policy was nurtured by the desire for work rationalisation. Implementation strategy however is not wholly determined by technology, for there is always an element of choice in how organisations set about introducing or upgrading their systems. To the naive observer there appears no such choice: the force of technology is such that it will inevitably dictate the shape and structure of the organisation and, by definition all activities within it, including implementation. Such an approach is entitled 'technological determinism'.

Broadly speaking there are three elements to the technological determinism argument. The first is that technology develops according to its own laws, quite independently from any social and cultural constraints. The march is inexorable. Second, if technology is to benefit society its development must not be hindered by any other considerations, save those of engineers, technicians and technocrats. The third is that the structure of an organisation is dictated by its technology. Joan Woodward is the researcher most associated with the technological determination argument, for in her 1958 survey of Essex (UK) firms she found a linear and curvilinear relationship between her particular 'scale' of technology and subsequent organisational structure. Technology was, then, of determining importance. Although criticisms have been levelled at her pioneering research, particularly that her scale of 'technology' was in fact a scale of increasing smoothness of production rather than of increasing complexity or use of chips in production and management, the force of the technological determination argument lives on. It lives on in the belief that the manager or the decision-maker in reality has no direct control over what will happen after the implementation of new technology. In the field of manufacturing organisations Sorge *et al.* (1983) found that this was definitely not the case. Social intervention and social control over implementation processes were found to be quite common. Computer numerical control production technology itself was malleable;

in point of fact there was room for organisational decisions as to how w restructure, or even if to restructure at all. Buchanan and Boddy (1983) in their UK survey found that managers of implementation often had a profound say in control of all aspects of computerisation and in the structuring of work. We return to examine this theme in chapter 4.

2.9 CHOICE OF IMPLEMENTATION STRATEGY

The reality of organisational life for many people in the past has been that systems have been implemented by 'experts'. The technocrat's day was at last seen to have come. The systems consultant, the manufacturer's representative, the systems analyst are but a few among many such experts party to implementation decisions. When we examine the choices available now, and in the future, we can see that choice of implementation strategy can be contingent on, among other things, the type of user analysis and the extent to which it precedes design, together with the level of user participation in system design. Bjorn-Anderson (1986) identifies four major implementation strategies, illustrated in Figure 2.2.

The expert can implement a system based solidly on Taylorist principles. It can be assured that the system selected will be labour saving, reduce workloads, produce the product more easily and result in faster working practices. Computer implementation can thus be seen as simply replacing outdated methods and machinery. This may well have been the case with, say, the advent of word processors: the typewriter was simply perceived as worn out, outdated.

But times have changed. Software has evolved to the point where

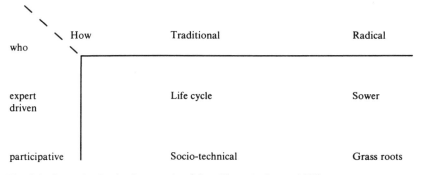

Fig. 2.2. Strategies for implementation (after Bjorn-Anderson 1986).

specific applications packages can now be bought off-the-shelf to solve particular problems. A shell system can be adapted, a hardware supplier can 'tailor' a product to unique organisational specifications. In essence, though, the strategy is still expert-driven. The human expert, after a diagnostic period of long or short duration (usually highly expensive) simple 'drops in' the system. As for any seed, the subsequent germination and flowering depend on environmental and, as is often the case, entirely fortuitous factors. The totally expert-driven system is a hit-or-miss affair and the essentially chance nature of the approach might remind us of the parable of the sower in the Bible.

Participative approaches to implementation can be divided into traditional and radical. The sociotechnical systems approach is best exemplified in the work of Mumford (1971). This approach does just what its label says: it attempts a synthesis between the best of the traditional life-cycle or Taylorist approach, so beloved of businesses, with a genuine recognition of the social and human needs of the operators. It is a prime example of the age-old beloved English art of compromise applied to the computer age. The governing feature of the sociotechnical systems approach lies in the attempt to establish a good 'fit' between the dual components of the social and the technical systems. If the technical system develops without reference to social needs and abilities, for example if it is of too advanced a level for the workforce or they are ill-trained, then troubles will inevitably ensue. The obverse is true. The social system itself must be in congruence with the technical system.

The most radical approach lies in the 'grass roots' method. Here the end users of the system carefully analyse their own needs and set about selecting the most useful hardware and software accordingly. On the face of it it seems an attractive proposition, and one not without a great deal of current cultural support. One advocate typical of the approach is Lucas (1982), who graphically relates the pitfalls of user resistance and lack of executive sponsorship of systems. The way out, he argues, is to involve users actively in the design process and also to seek top-down support. It is, as we shall examine later in the chapter, a controversial approach, not least because of the conflicting results of empirical research into its actual effectiveness, and also for political reasons. The approach has been cynically dubbed by its critics as 'post-industrial syndicalism', for a situation could in practice arise where users select a system which, whilst suited to their own sectarian ends, is hopelessly out of touch with overall organisational goals.

2.10 ORGANISATIONAL VARIABLES AND IMPLEMENTATION

Whoever becomes the main instigator of systems implementation must have a thorough understanding of all the variables likely to affect it before any strategy is chosen. It is a moot point whether such a global, holistic and educated viewpoint is distributed among end users. Why should this be? The literature is replete with examples where inadequate analysis of crucial organisational variables and slavish adherence to an inappropriate strategy has resulted in disasters. In the author's experience, most companies approached can relate at least one catastrophe. For our purposes we can see the business organisation as dependent on the relationship between the task (what is done), the technology (how it is done) and the people who undertake it. The mutual dependency of these four variables is illustrated in Figure 2.3.

In Figure 2.3 the inner circle would be the type of bureaucratic organisation where a large volume of work of a routine nature is undertaken and where the resultant organisational structure is rigid and bureaucratic. State and government bureaucracies together with banking and insurance are such examples. These are often characterised by what Deal and Kennedy (1982) term a 'process culture': a culture where doing things by the book, covering your mistakes and keeping your copy-book clean are implicit organisational rules. Although stars or entrepreneurs are found within this culture, generally low-risk, routine work results in a

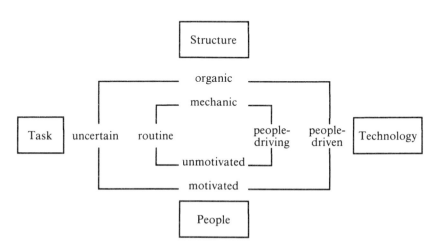

Fig. 2.3. Mutual dependency of organisational variables (after Bjorn-Anderson 1986).

relatively unmotivated risk-aversive workforce. Perhaps the moves in the UK to privatise large government bureaucracies represent an assault on these inefficiencies. Many sectors of large-scale manufacturing (especially car manufacture) are like this.

Another major variable of organisational structure is the organic type of structure. Here the organisation is seen as being more flexible, more quick to respond to circumstances, with departments or subunits withering or flowering as the case may be. This basic distinction in organisational structure was much explored and researched in the 1960s and early 1970s (see Burns and Stalker 1961). In Figure 2.3 the outer circle represents organisations that are 'people-driven'; personnel are usually highly motivated and are operating in an uncertain world which is perhaps fast-moving: for example in research and development departments. It can exist in young firms in the consumer electronics sector (see Adamson & Kennedy 1986 for an analysis of Sinclair UK as a prototype). The traditional 'life-cycle' Taylorist approach would suit organisations in the inner circle. The more one moves towards the perimeter, the more user involvement and even radical 'grass roots' implementation strategies seem appropriate. Most probably though an amalgam of social-technical approaches and 'grass roots' would be suitable, though whatever path is chosen a holistic consideration of an organisation's task, structure, technology and people is paramount.

2.11 PRACTISING IMPLEMENTATION

Few organisational decision-makers sit down, plot the main variables and select an overall implementation strategy that best 'fits' their organisation. Not that the extant research literature can prescribe unequivocal recommendations for each type of organisation: manifestly it cannot. Because of the number of variables involved a prescriptive 'cook book' method is empirically, if not logically, impossible. All aspects of the organisation – the business, the future organisational shape, the markets present and future, the products, the people and so forth – all would have to be meticulously evaluated and a formula derived. Notwithstanding this, business practice, as usual in information technology, strides ahead of theory or model building. Technological determination has given way to management considering the wide choice of options open on implementation policies. Case studies, for example Rowe (1990), demonstrate this breadth of vision. So just what appears to be current business practice?

2.12 END USER MODELS AND IMPLEMENTATION PRACTICES

The 1980s saw a marked shift away from Taylorist approaches and concepts in favour of participative and democratic systems. Typical of these are appeals for adapting business software to suit user needs (for a description of the process see Floyd and Keil 1983). All of these approaches are drawing upon essentially psychological 'models' of the end user. People, it is argued, work better when involved in the design and implementation of systems. Systems are likely to be accepted by users if there has been an intimate consideration of human needs at every step of the planning and implementation process.

However, despite passionate pleas for user involvement the call often goes unheeded. Blackler and Brown (1986) surveyed UK practices and found that despite the expressed popularity of user involvement in design and implementation, little more than lip-service was paid to this in day-to-day business reality. Professionals in the field of human resource management – ergonomists, human factors experts and organisational psychologists – are all trained to survey user needs and to articulate and spell out their demands. Yet in the organisations surveyed by the authors in the UK their services were minimal or even absent. The authors rightly conclude though that people such as human factors experts and ergonomists are usually only marginal to high-level strategic decision-making when it comes to the implementations of systems. This 'expert advice' is called in, but it is by no means certain that it will be used. Ergonomists and human factors experts are consulted by the major hardware manufacturers at all stages of product development, and also by the software supply industry. In this field the human factors laboratory or its analogue is established business reality whose practical research output is widely respected (see IBM *Hursley Human Factors Laboratory Research Reports*).

The host organisation can often be seen to be lacking in such expertise. This state of affairs is a continuing source of dismay for many people, not least for those persons concerned with raising the professional profile of ergonomists and human factors experts. Relative costs to the organisation of implementation have changed dramatically over the past few years. Organisational costs of implementation – training, retraining, possible relocation costs, even organisational restructuring costs – now constitute by far the major part of expenditure. 'Orgware', as it is known, is the total cost of organisational implementation. Since staff are expensive (and increasingly difficult to find due to demographic factors) and likely to become more expensive still, we can easily see why the orgware bill is high and likely to climb higher. By contrast, the price of hardware is plummeting and software costs are steadily being pushed down (see Rowe 1990).

2.13 END USER IDEOLOGY

Assumptions about what is the best approach to any aspect of organisational change, whether technology-based or not, when made by non-experts are usually based on current fashion or dominant ideology. The hard-headed businessman will reach for a solution that has been seen to be already used, tried, tested and adopted by other organisations. By far the major part of everyday business decision-making at corporate level is not concerned with ferreting out the innovative, the untried, the daring. It is not concerned with unearthing the bold or novel sweeping solution. That way involves too much risk, especially when huge sums of money are involved as is the case with anything to do with information technology. Business decision-making is concerned with doing the same things well, or doing them better than before in a predictable, smooth, regular way. This sentiment is captured wonderfully by Sampson (1973) who recounts the favourite phrase of Howard Geneen, head of ITT, when he regularly assembled the heads of divisions normally scattered over the four corners of the globe. He preceeded each meeting with the solemn words 'I want no surprises'.

Pressure exists then to follow the herd, to make pragmatic decisions guided by the common-sense wisdom of established business practice. Let other people make the errors. May you be the party to benefit by their mistakes. The answer to pithy problems of implementation must, it is argued, lie in the simple truths of everyday practice.

The dominant ideology guiding many planners is that user involvement is absolutely necessary. It constitutes an article of faith that guides many planners and can be seen to underpin much thinking and model-building. People will accept systems better and will be less likely to

Phases	TASK AND TECHNOLOGY CENTRED APPROACH Guiding assumptions and key actors	ORGANISATION AND END-USER CENTRED APPROACH Guiding assumptions and key actors
1 INITIAL REVIEW	Operating conditions People are a costly resource to be reduced if possible Key actors: top and senior managers	Operating conditions People are a costly resource to be more fully utilised Key actors: initially from any part of the organisation, then top management
2 EXPLORATION AND PRIOR JUSTIFICATION	Tightly prescribed planning objectives Central coordination and control Expert driven 'Most modern' syndrome Key actors: managerial project team including technical and financial experts	General policy formulation Decentralisation, staff involvement Concern for end users System development potential rather than machine capability Key actors: representative group, consulting project group. Trade union involvement
3 DESIGN OF SYSTEM	Machines over people Task fragmentation 'Clean design' 'Final design' Key actors: design engineers and technical consultants	People to use machines Job enrichment, teams Operator and maintenance needs Incremental and educative design approach Key actors: design engineers, technical consultants, behavioural advisers
4 IMPLEMENTATION	Machine capability Only minor modifications expected 'Once off' skill training Responsibility to line management Key actors: as phase 3, also line managers and end-users. Trade union negotiations on conditions	User support Pilot projects used where possible Continuing staff and organisation development Continuing reviews of operation and needs Key actors: as phase 3 also line managers and end-users. Trade unions

Fig. 2.4. Alternative style of planning and assumptions of planner (adapted from Blackler and Brown 1987).

resist implementation if they are genuine parties to decisions surrounding it. Blackler and Brown (1987) identify two major models: the 'task and technology' approach and the 'organisation or end user centred' approach. The task and technology approach corresponds roughly to our Taylorist approach previously identified, while the organisational, end user approach is a participative, flexible human-centred approach. These two contrasting models are illustrated in Figure 2.4.

The authors adopt a four-phase approach to implementation (for consideration of alternative descriptive phases see Allgera & Koopman 1984). The first stage is what we term the initial review or the first recognition of a potential for computerisation/update. The second stage is labelled the exploration and prior justification phase; this usually involves the extended analysis of feasibility. The next stage involves the planners in the design of the system (the detailing or tailoring of packages or selection of software). Finally the actual implementation is reached. This is the installation, trials and mode of implementation (for instance parallel systems or 'big bang' switchover). The driving force throughout the four phases is that user involvement is the touchstone of success.

The assumption, and it is an assumption, that the participation approach is the best one can however be put to empirical test. Do organisations that actively engage users in systems design and implementation actually outperform those competitors who instead shun user involvement? Ives and Olsen (1984), in a meticulously-researched and hard-hitting paper, point out that the drive for participation by end users is historically the tail end of the drive for employee participation once so prevalent in the 1970s. The writers, academics and researchers who advocate participation almost as an unquestioned article of faith may be guilty of particularism here for they are viewing the world through their own experience. Most likely, the argument runs, they were college educated during the late 1960s and 1970s. Demand for participation in decision-making among undergraduate bodies was then at its most passionate and most vocal. They carried forward with them into research and writing the 'Holy Grail' of participation (see Wall & Lischeron 1977 for a flavour of this thinking).

Ives and Olsen studied what happened when management information systems were introduced, using participative end user driven techniques. Of the 22 cases studied only a miserly eight showed a positive relationship between user participation and ultimate business success! Seven results were equivocal and seven showed negative conditions or were otherwise not statistically significant. The authors attack the fashionable calls for user involvement, together with many of the so-called research papers 'proving' the utility of user involvement, saying that much of the existing research is poorly grounded in theory and is seriously methodologically flawed. User involvement has crept into management thinking via the discipline of organisational behaviour and in particular the study of group problem solving. Here laboratory studies supposedly show that participative decision-making techniques increase the input of subordinates. Studies conducted in the context of organisations are at best equivocal. Lock and Schweiger (1979) in a thorough survey found ambiguous evidence for a relationship between participation and any improvements in productivity (which included the quality of decision-making). There was however some evidence that participation increased job satisfaction, particularly in the area of people accepting organisational change. But can one argue from participation studies to active user involvement in implementation? The answer is yes, if one views the process of end user involvement in system implementation as a subset of participation in decision-making. At heart of course are strong feelings of democratic rights to be invoked at the work place. Since we are committed to democracy as a political ideal, it seems morally right that it should extend down to shop floor working life. More devastating it is then when research findings such as these demonstrate that such long-cherished beliefs bear little truth when scrutinised.

But exactly what is user participation supposed to do? Ives and Olsen claim believers have blind faith in a number of outcomes:

- User involvement can give a more real assessment of the information requirements of users.
- Unacceptable or unimportant features will not be developed if users are carefully consulted.
- Users will necessarily develop a better understanding of the system by being consulted.

Participation will generate user acceptance by the simple fact that during participation exercises users will understand better the system capabilities, grievances will be aired, fears can be ventilated and commitment can therefore be developed to the full.

Much of the research on user involvement does appear flawed simply because of measurement difficulties. Ives and Olsen point out that the best possible indicator we will have of the success or otherwise of a computer-based information system is the total economic benefit accruing to it when it is compared with alternative investments. Clearly this is not on. We cannot freeze the march of business while we examine it. The intense pressure to computerise, often results in an 'automate or liquidate' mentality within the organisation (Winfield 1986). This was the case during the economic stringencies and business recession which accompanied much of the wave of computerisation in the UK during the 1980s.

In surveys of organisations the actual relationship between user involvement and system success can easily be overstated. Research studies and surveys frequently employ *ex post facto* measures of user involvement, which presents the likelihood that a 'halo effect' will influence results. The actual success or failure of system implementation will undoubtedly affect users' perceptions of their involvement in its development. If it fails nobody wants to be associated with it; if it is a runaway success all wish to bask in the limelight.

But lack of user participation, or token or pseudo participation, can have effects on organisations that are difficult but not impossible to quantify. One effect is hurt feelings: the feeling of being ignored or of having been snubbed when implementation is undertaken without any concern for users. One senior database editor spoke in the following disparaging terms about her experience at a large publishing house.

'One morning without any advance warning Wang PCs arrived on every desk in the organisation. We had at the time no explanation of where they came from, what they were to be used for, or whatever. For a year they lay mostly unused, save for trivial purposes, on people's desks. We learned that the boss had done a deal with the supplier. No attempt at explanation or training was offered or given, no help or outside contacts were given. The potential that was thrown away for enlisting staff goodwill by that one silly act was enormous. Of course some people familiarised themselves with the hardware and available software but underuse was terrific. As an implementation policy it defied explanation.'

Another worker in a specialist automobile parts company tells a different story.

'The boss employed a programmer part-time for over a year to develop the software for the ordering, goods inwards, stock levels and so on. It came to nothing. It became something of a joke among staff because the programmer was obviously working full time somewhere else and doing our job as a 'foreigner'. He was the phantom who arrived at night after we had all gone home. The boss has now finally decided to do the job thoroughly. An organisation and methods consultant is now working on the system with flow diagrams, organising the paperwork into proper data capture format and so forth. We are all co-operating in the switchover of course but there has not been any detailed participation, sitting round a table discussing, explaining, that sort of thing. Partly I suppose it is because we are only a small outfit (and likely to be smaller still when the system is up and running). The main reason for the lack of participation is that at the end of the day there is so little choice. Seen from the outside, it all seems so cut and dried. There is no pioneering work to be done. You buy the hardware and software – the choice is fairly limited in this specialist area – and you implement it. All I have been asked to do so far is comment on the appropriateness of a few forms.'

A few months after implementation the worker's disparaging account continues:

'Choice of "D" day was an unmitigating disaster. He (the boss) could not have picked a worse time. It was just after Christmas, bang in the middle of sales. All items in stock had a new price, there were new ways of calculating discounts, everything. And all the time we had to contend with the new system. Oh yes we were given training in the new system alright – fifteen minutes' introduction, if you could credit it by that name. To make matters worse the training session had to come out of our own time. You had to stay behind after everyone else had gone home. Miss the bus and stand in the rain.'

Loss of goodwill and lowered staff morale make themselves felt through poor working atmosphere and subsequent high turnover. Turbulence costs the organisation money. It thus seems that if staff see participation as important, then make no mistake it most certainly is. It is however a foolhardy organisation that will rush in thinking that it is always an absolute necessity.

2.14 WHO IS SUCCESSFUL AT IMPLEMENTATION?

Another approach to studying implementation strategies is to try to fit approaches into broad models or styles. This approach seeks not to demonstrate the worth of a particular approach, instead it attempts to be studiously value-neutral. It simply observes what happens neutrally, dispassionately and ignores or minimises grand theory building. In implementing new technology most decision-makers are not likely to be driven by particular ideologies, nor do they have particular axes to grind. They are likely to be unashamedly eclectic in approach, in just the same way that they are likely to be eclectic in their approach to job design. For all intents and purposes they will ignore or be unaware of the prescriptions, guidelines or exhortations for the currently fashionable. 'Guidelines' are offered by researchers and authors who, far from being dispassionate observers, often themselves posses a political and ethical drum to beat. Business practice though reacts adversely to high-minded exhortations: historically the businessman distrusts the pulpit. To pursue the analogy with job redesign further, the high claims made for job redesign based on essentially ethical principles may have directly promoted a more sober, atheoretical approach among businessmen. As Buchanan (1987) shows, in the design of high performance work stations credence is given to sound human relations values such as the encouragement of skills development, creativity and flexibility, but these are allied strongly to long-term market objectives and the strategic use of new technology.

Brenda Wroe (1985) studied small to medium sized companies in the UK construction industry. As an industrial sector it underuses computer-based management information systems, even though many of its business activities (requisitions, ordering, supplies, critical path analysis, transport deployment and so on) seem ripe for computer mediation. In chapter 6 we examine the role of information technology in strategic decisions in these and other sectors. Wroe concluded that the experience of small companies with implementation is qualitatively different from the experience of large organisations. Extrapolations cannot be made from large organisations to guide implementation in small organisations. Perhaps a taxonomy of experiences based upon variables such as sector and size would be useful here. Wroe found, in her small sample of case histories of implementation, that often the only predictor variable for success or failure was the managing director's knowledge of, and enthusiasm for, computers. To use a disease analogy, he was the infector agent that infected the whole organisation top-down. As noted earlier in this chapter, her survey found less than perfect success with implementation. Her approach is neutral, not looking for examples to fit a theory or support a cause. She simply isolated those variables that differentiated firms with successful implementation outcomes from firms with unsuccessful outcomes. Wroe used a three-phase implementation system: selection, implementation and live operation. In the selection phase, successful companies:

- had more than adequate financial support
- had a clear identification of the potential problem areas and overall company objectives
- undertook a thorough feasibility assessment
- possessed highly committed staff
- engaged senior managers to undertake a detailed review of the computing market with a detailed breakdown of their information requirements at their disposal
- drew on outside contacts, consultants and advisers (though most interestingly the companies reported difficulties in locating these)

In the implementation phase successful companies:

- established close contacts with the system supplier; they demanded and received a high level of support from them
- were highly disciplined in approach to implementation, for instance they thought through synchronisation and dual operation of the manual and computer systems well in advance
- found the training and long-term support was poor from the suppliers due mainly to the intense competiveness of the microcomputer market in a volatile period; many had simply gone out of business
- used a certain amount of organisational slack or spare labour to support the system
- opted for proven packaged software in preference to in-house software development
- timed implementation to match the financial year

During the live operation phase successful companies:

- started off with restricted operation to ensure full controlled development
- established a sound relationship with the supplier (one supplier used a successful company as a reference site)
- quickly transferred operating responsibility to a trained assistant who could devote full attention to the system

Unsuccessful companies proceeded radically differently, for in the selection phase:

- they were in an insecure financial position, many of them experiencing cash-flow problems
- the 'trigger' for the system came not from within the company but from outside
- they had little outside help and support: each unsuccessful company evaluated only one commercial system beforehand
- managers had a strong craft- or production-orientated background, they possessed unrealistically high expectations of the system's capabilities

During the implementation phase unsuccessful companies:

- were unable to draft personnel in to resource the system; problems became particularly acute when the two systems operated in parallel
- did no planning for the participation of 'externals' with the system, for example accountants
- were frequently not even up to date on the operation of the present system and therefore crucial data were unavailable for capture by the new system
- were unable to offer training due to constraints on staff time

Survey findings such as these are helpful for system implementers in that they may alert them to possible pitfalls in their own implementation processes. Their value increases however as the firms surveyed in the literature come closer in activity, size, environment and so on to their own. However, only a limited amount of extrapolation can be made from the experience of construction firms to other sectors.

2.15 USER NEEDS FOR OFFICE SYSTEMS SOLUTIONS

Who is going to be brave enough to gaze into the crystal ball and to predict future user needs, when it is difficult enough to ascertain user needs at the present point in time? Systems analysts have a cynical saying along the lines: 'What users ask for is not what they want, and what they want is not what they need'. In the same vein Bair (1987) remarks 'When office workers are asked about their wants, they are disposed towards what is currently popular; manufacturers must respond to popularity with products that are only part of the solution'. Bair attacks market research methods undertaken by manufacturers as part of that very problem. Market research, he argues, concentrates on wants: immediate, perceived, obvious. The market survey is often conducted by questionnaire; often by direct observation of office behaviour. What does the observer see in offices? He sees traffic, interruptions in the work flow, queues at the photocopier. If, argues the researcher, we probe deeper and analyse (perhaps by extended interview or counselling, towards the interpretive end of the spectrum in Figure 2.1) we see that people want work solutions essentially at the workgroup level. Since most work needs are related to communication and since communication occurs within the primary working group, then the solution to the problem must needs be at the workgroup level. Bair interprets the distinction between user needs and user wants in the following way. User wants are specific desires and requests, usually confined to specific items of technology. Wants can be seen as analogous to the wants of a child for a particular toy: they reflect current inadequacies rather than mature, future solutions. User needs are related to general problems; they can only come about by a thorough analysis of the job.

The bold step the author takes is to claim that the crucial next stage in implementation of office systems will revolve around needs at the work group level. These needs will be driven by the desire for connectivity between co-workers. A simple technological fix like reducing time spent on typing may be preferred to making sweeping changes in how people work together. At heart is the distinction between the efficient organisation and the effective one. Work can be super efficient but to no useful business end. It is effective work if it furthers total business ends. The net gain to so many organisations of the incremental Taylorist efficiency approach to office automation has been zero. The concept of work efficiency is individualistic. The concept of effectiveness is, by contrast, social for it applies to groups and how they work together; how they pull together for the good of the company. Users, it is argued, are becoming aware of the shortcomings of personal computers. Feelings of isolation and personal alienation are issues we shall address in later chapters.

Connectivity needs arise because workers are becoming aware of the importance of information sharing. The effective organisation looks at the totality of people working together as a team: people even if efficient are not isolated individuals, for teamwork and social connectivity count for much more. People thus need access to file-sharing systems; they would like to have 'transparent databases' where nobody has a property relation to some remote database, because it is everywhere, accessible by everyone. All can use and manipulate the database. Access to a common file, to facilitate multiple authorship, and shared screen teleconferencing, whereby two people can change the screen content regardless of location, will be future demands. Some even argue that there is something of a cultural change taking place among the young: computer literate from an early age they regard information access as an inalienable right. They want to be free to roam databases, be they corporate or worldwide. It is an iconoclastic vision, based on dismantling rigid hierarchies of access and knowledge. The hacker breaking into information stores is not seen as deviant, but as romantic hero pushing back the boundaries of what is shareable. This new cultural movement may be more talked about and written about than real, but in the US it has been labelled already. The heady synthesis of punk values and culture and cybernetics yields the title 'cyberpunk culture'.

Is the desire for communication and shared information able to stand up to empirical scrutiny? Bair's survey was based on 691 'knowledge workers' in US offices where it was found that on average 48% of face-to-face communication was within the workgroup. Clearly compositions of workgroups in offices vary according to structure, type of work, size and so on, but the findings were that workgroups tend to be coincidental with the departmental unit with, on average, 10–20 professionals reporting to a single manager. Smaller taskgroups, say of five to eight people, exist within the department and naturally within such groups interpersonal communication is even higher. With the increased focus on the department as a cost centre, implementation in the future may be actively forced into giving genuine credence to the social dimension of work. Effective groupworking must then be the next emergent organisational goal, a conclusion reached as early as 1985 by Strassman who reviewed extensive consultancy experience in this field.

2.16 EVALUATING TECHNOLOGY

The main thrust of this chapter has been on examining implementation and the management of change mainly in office environments. Business and operating environments quite naturally influence this process profoundly. We have not dealt at length on the different pressures facing, say, service and manufacturing organisations to implement. These are multiple and complex and deserving of textbooks in their own right. Recently (see for example Clegg *et al.* 1988; McKerrow 1988) there appears to be a body of opinion which believes that information technology can be evaluated for its total worth to the organisation. Guidelines have been drawn up as to how to conduct such evaluation exercises, exercises it might be added which can be conducted in the organisation be it manufacturing, service, finance, leisure or otherwise.

Clegg *et al.* (1988) suggest that all successful evaluations are based on seven propositions.

(1) Evaluation should concern all tasks to be done, not merely the computer system. The focus should be on the total objectives of the department or company and not simply the piece of hardware that is supposed to support these objectives. The authors warn us that the quest for efficiency results in tunnel vision – a point noted earlier in this chapter. Increased effectiveness should be the goal to judge things by.

(2) Evaluation should be orientated to action. This means that one should not start the evaluation exercise itself unless actually prepared to change things. Again the overall objective is improved performance.

(3) Evaluation should be systematic. All assumptions should be tested and the evaluation exercise involve as small a number of personnel as possible, working to a planned timetable.

(4) The exercise should be prepared to delve beyond the most obvious and pressing problems. Naturally it should be given the resources to do so.

(5) Evaluation should be participative, enlisting as wide a degree of expertise and support as possible. Interpretation of the results should be participative too.

(6) The evaluation should be comparative: benchmarks must be chosen for standards of comparison, competitors' performances should be noted and assessment made of whether the kit meets its published standards of performance.

(7) The evaluation exercise must itself be tailor made to suite local needs.

To help ascertain whether the system meets essential requirements the authors reproduce screening questionnaires. Respondents have to assess whether, for example, there are major or minor problems with meeting business goals, coping with anticipated future needs or linking together different sets of data. Respondents are asked what are the best and worst aspects of the equipment in use, what improvements they would like to see and so on. Assessment of the overall usability of the system is similarly surveyed, as are job quality and performance together with organisational aspects of effectiveness.

2.17 RESISTANCE TO IMPLEMENTATION

The literature on human resistance to organisational change, whether computer-based or not, is replete with horror stories. People will react to change with all manner of deviant, disturbed and often entertaining behaviours. Why should this be? What does the organisation come to represent such that it elicits all manner of anti-social behaviour? The organisation at the economic level buys people's labour. The only formal relationship people have with an employing organisation is simply an exchange one. At a deeper level, however, the organisation comes to represent in the mind of the employee all manner of weird and wonderful things (see Winfield 1984). It becomes benevolent friend, even protecting parent; it becomes an internalised set of values; it comes to represent a valued way of life. On the other hand it can become feared and hated. It can be seen as hated impersonal dictator or harsh autocratic slave-driver; as despised parent, real or imaginary. It is the stuff of fairy stories.

The deeper meanings the organisation and its bosses come to have are neatly explained by psychoanalytic theory and a whole genre of business writing on this theme awaits the curious student. No more readable example can be found than in the work of Kets de Vries (Kets de Vries 1980; Kets de Vries & Millar 1984). What behaviours do people demonstrate during unwanted change? They display aggression (often far beyond what is warranted); they will project or offload onto the organisation all manner of feelings and attributes. They can claim that it is out to destroy them, that it is out to humiliate them, that it is out to make them old before their time – the catalogue is endless. But as a last resort they will turn to the oldest trick in the book: avoidance. They will simply refuse to entertain the thought of change and find instead all manner of often bizarre diversionary activities.

If we examine resistance to implementation the first thing that strikes us is the near uniformity of public behaviours the resistors will use. To a person they will all show hostility. Hirshheim and Newman (1988) take an interesting model when they explain this hostility. It is a model derived in part from the psychoanalytic thinking of Sigmund Freud. They argue that the overt displays of hostility mask deeper fears. Hostility, so the argument runs, is always bred from frustration. Frustration, as we all know, in turn is fuelled by conflict. Conflict comes from the fact that at the core of ourselves we see some threat to the satisfaction of our human needs. So there you have it. If you feel unloved or rejected it's because of those infernal machines, the computers.

Deviant and disturbed behaviour surrounding computer use and implementation is a fascinating area to explore and the repressed delinquent can gain vicarious thrills by reading about all manner of documented computer wrecking. What is the quickest way to wreck a mainframe armed only with a handfull of paperclips? Do you know just how easy it is to create a computer virus more virulent and unstoppable than AIDS? What is the cook-book method for cracking codes and passwords? Did you know how easy it is to trick your ATM into dishing out more money than it should?

The Luddites were 19th-century machine wreckers. It is commonly believed they were simply anti-machine peasants. In fact they were a nascent industrial working class fearful of the loss of wages and collective bargaining rights that the machines came to represent to them. Later on in the era of the mechanical assembly belt the 'spanner in the works' did the equivalent: it brought the line and the whole machine to a grinding halt.

It appears then that every technological advance provokes an equal and opposite destructive force: people learn to become ever more ingenious and devious in their ways of screwing the system up. Hackers, computer fraudsters and system wreckers might be the only genuine anarchists left, and anarchists are like death-watch beetles, quietly ticking away whilst all around them rush headlong into their monied 'yuppie' utopias.

At the level of the workaday world people will withhold data deliberately; they will even deliberately provide inaccurate data; they will show lowered morale and express ill-feeling. The author was related the story of how one financial manager in the brewing industry so thoroughly distrusted the computer printout of the company's financial position that he pored over the figures, checking and rechecking for three whole days and nights. He even took the figures home and 'burnt the midnight oil' on the task. Computer distrust takes strange forms.

Many commentators have documented the changing nature of resistance as the implementation cycle progresses. Taking a three-phase cycle of implementation, during the systems analysis phase users will simply be unwilling to take part in the requirements specification. It can, and indeed does, drive systems analysts to drink and despair – it drives some poor souls to even more desperate measures. But then again is this not exactly what the resistors want? During the implementation phase proper, users will take no interest or fail to come forward to fill roles during the actual system introduction. Call a meeting of users or representatives and vast legions of personnel are mysteriously absent: on sick leave, away visiting, tied up in life-or-death meetings, having emergency dental treatment. In the final phase, the live operation phase, blank refusal to co-operate can take place, as can distrust, absenteeism and high labour turnover. Organisations need to be aware that the negative features of implementation can often be high labour turnover, leading to unsatisfactory levels of organisational turbulence among what are, after all, key personnel.

What of the argument that people will always resist change; fight tooth and nail against anything that upsets their routine? To take our Machiavelli quote as an established truth about society leads one to rather despairing conclusions. We would forever be locked in habit, afraid to change, venture forth and try the new. People *will* opt for the new, *will* break out of old moulds, unfetter themselves from the shackles of tradition. On a societal scale the events in Eastern Europe during the closing weeks of 1989 and the opening months of 1990 bear witness to this. The 'innate conservatism' view of people just will not hold water. At the level of the implementation of systems people will claim they have no need for the system – does this then reveal their conservatism? No, one can say that they simply have not been convinced. Certainly there is plenty of evidence, anecdotal and case history, that active involvement and participation in change leads to subsequent commitment. The reality is that resistant people need a gentle nudge in order for them to become involved in the first place. They are often paralysed with anxiety. They know deep down that with computerisation comes a redistribution of resources. They know they will eventually have to defend their territory, even draw up battle lines or plan expansionary moves. Budgets will change, their allocation and distribution will change. All sorts of hardware and equipment will be up for grabs. Staff, resources, even physical territory will be in the melting pot. Since information is power, authority and hence access to career ladders may all seem to be up for grabs too.

Common sense in management suggests a few rules to follow in order to minimise the possible emergence of resistance. In themselves the rules are nothing new: they can be derived from the pragmatics of the Human Relations school of management thought quite easily. Sensible management would invest time and money 'selling' the system by the usual 'massage' of seminars, illustrated talks, role play exercises and such like – user involvement being the overriding guiding principle. Another ploy would be, wherever possible, to build a prototype, get it up and running and then train people carefully. The transition to electronic trading in the City of London – 'Big Bang' – was smoothed by several well orchestrated dry runs. One tenet of good organisational communication, whatever the issue, is to break things down into manageable digestible portions. In implementation terms it means breaking the system down into manageable 'chunks' or descriptive units which people can easily comprehend. Man as a limited information processor is a theme adopted readily in software design and it can usefully be applied at the organisational level too.

All this can only be done by effective strategic decision-making and leadership. A senior level appointment therefore needs to be made. His or her remit will be to negotiate with users, oversee the 'selling' of the system and steer policy planning committees through the jungle of delegation problems. Hopefully they will see that formal contracts of commitment are forthcoming from people and that non-productive territory games and destructive counterproductive power struggles and personality clashes will be minimised if not headed off altogether. Part of the 'massage' act will be to let people know that interesting and challenging work will ensue from computerisation. If systems staff are trained to appreciate the importance of organisational effect then they can be important allies here. The adoption of a 'soft systems' methodology discussed in chapter 4 is a great help here.

2.18 CONCLUSION

To implement information technology wisely needs a thorough consideration of all aspects of the business context, together with a thorough review of the feasible solution set. Two main questions have to be squarely tackled.

First is participation going to be an option at all? System designers will have to consider carefully the negative findings about the relationship of participation and its effect on system quality, system usage, user attitudes and on user satisfaction with the information thus received. Is participation going to be genuine and undertaken in an atmosphere of mutual trust and co-operation? If there is only one design option, and for many systems there is only one option feasible, then participation may in fact be a non-starter. In these circumstances it has to be restricted to a few narrow areas where there is latitude for influence. The tone and climate in which the exercise is conducted then become all important, especially so to the end users.

The second point is that there is a trade-off between the benefits of user involvement in time and cost. If a system has to be implemented with any degree of urgency, participation will definitely slow things down. Basic questions will have to be asked about the workforce. For example do they actually need to be self-directed beings? Do they need to be aware of the reasons for a particular choice? Do they need to be able to understand the reasons behind a particular design decision? Will ignorance suffice?

If participation is to be pursued then the form of representation will have to be worked out long in advance. Hedberg and Mumford (1975) noted that often representatives of users end up in one of two positions during negotiations. The first is what he calls the 'hostage position'. Here the representative is usually ill informed on technical matters. He or she does not want to appear such and, as a consequence, takes very little part in discussions. The representative takes few risks, asks few pertinent questions and consequently has little influence on the overall design. The second position is what he terms the 'indoctrination alternative'. There has to be an educational process undertaken before the representative can understand the concepts and language used by the systems designers. This takes place over time and he or she eventually ends up speaking the same language as systems people. But when the representative comes to communicate with the people whom he or she represents, difficulties arise in translating back and explaining the crucial concepts. The mass of the workforce then think that the representative has come to think more and more like the system designers and less like them. The net result is that the representative becomes alienated from the very people he or she is entrusted to represent.

Often a 'political' solution is sought to participation. In practice this often means that representatives will be selected and advanced who are suitable to the designers. Subtle alliances between influential persons, opinion leaders and informal leaders will be carefully (and quite cynically) nurtured. The whole area becomes a delicate network of influence, of checks and balances, of horse-trading and collusion. The setting, rightly speaking, is squarely in the field of industrial relations. Machiavelli still lives.

2.19 REFERENCES

Adamson I. & Kennedy R. (1986) *Sinclair and the 'Sunrise' Technology*. Penguin Books, Harmondsworth.

Allgera J.A. & Koopman P. (1984) Automation design process and implementation. In *Handbook of Work and Organisational Psychology* (Ed. by P.J.D. Drenth, H. Thiery, P.J. Willems & C.J. de Wolff). Wiley, Chichester.

Aziz K. (1986) *So You Think Your Business Needs A Computer?* Kogan Page, London.

Bair J.H. (1987) User needs for office systems solutions. In *Technology and the Transformation of White Collar Work* (Ed. by R.E. Kraut). Erlbaum, London.

Bjorn-Anderson N. (1986) Implementation of office systems. In *Office Systems* (Ed. by A.A. Verrign-Stuart & R. Hirschheim). North Holland, Amsterdam.

Blackler F. & Brown C. (1986) Current British practices in the evaluation of the new information technologies. In *Proceedings of the West European Conference on the Psychology of Work and Organisations* (Ed. by H.W. Schroiff & G. Debus). North Holland, Amsterdam.

Blackler F. & Brown C. (1987) Management, organisations and the new technologies. In *Information Technology and People* (Ed. by F. Blackler & D. Oborne). Macmillan, London.

Buchanan D. (1987) Job enrichment is dead: long live high-performance work design. *Personnel Management*, May, 40–3.

Buchanan D. & Boddy D. (1983) *Organisations in the Computer Age*. Gower Press, Aldershot.

Burns T. & Stalker S.M. (1961) *The Management of Innovation*. Tavistock, London.

Clegg C. *et al.* (1988) *People and Computers: How to Evaluate Your Company's New Technology*. Ellis Horwood, Chichester.

Damoderam L. (1986) Human factors in office systems. In *Office Systems* (Ed. by A.A. Verrign-Stuart & R. Hirschheim). North Holland, Amsterdam.

Deal T.E. & Kennedy A.E. (1982) *Organisational Culture: The Rites and Rituals of Corporate life*. Addison Wesley, New York.

Emery F.E. (1969) *Systems Thinking*. Penguin Books, Harmondsworth.

Floyd C. & Keil R. (1983) Adapting software development for systems design with users. In *Systems Design: By, For and With Users* (Ed. by U. Briefs, C. Ciborra & L. Scheider). North Holland, Amsterdam.

Gorge A., Hartmann G. & Warner G. (1983) *Microelectronics and Manpower in Manufacturing: Applications of Computer Numerical Control in Great Britain and West Germany*. Gower, Aldershot.

Greer G. (1984) *Sex and Destiny*. Secker and Warberg, London.

Habermas J. (1980) *Critical Social Theory*. Hutchinson, London.

Hedberg B. & Mumford E. (1975) Computer systems to support industrial democracies. In *Human Choice and Computers* (Ed. by E. Mumford & H. Sackmann). North Holland, Amsterdam.

Hirschheim R. (1985) *Office Automation: a Social and Organisational Perspective*. Wiley, Chichester.

Hirschheim R. (1986) Perspectives and views of the office: alternative approaches to understanding the office. In *Office Systems* (Ed. by A.A. Verrijn-Stuart & R. Hirschheim). North Holland, Amsterdam.

Hirschheim R. & Feeny D.F. (1986) Experiences with office automation, some lessons and recommendations. *Journal of General Management*, 12(2), 25–40.

Hirschheim R. & Newman M. (1988) Information systems and user resistance: theory and practice. *The Computer Journal*, 31(5), 398–408.

IBM *Hursley Human Factors Laboratory Research Reports*. IBM, Hursley Park, Winchester, UK.

Ives B. & Olsen M.H. (1984) User involvement and MIS success: a review of research. *Management Science*, 30(5), 586–603.

Kets de Vries M.F.R. (1980) *Organisational Paradoxes: Clinical Approaches to Management*. Tavistock, London.

Kets de Vries M.F.R. & Millar M. (1984) *The Neurotic Organisation: Diagnosing and Changing Counter Productive Styles of Management*. Jossey-Bass, San Francisco.

Lock E.A. & Schweiger D.M. (1979) Participation in decision-making. One more look. *Research in Organisational Behaviour*, 1, 265–339.

Lucas H.C. (1982) *Information System Concepts for Management*, 2nd edn. McGraw Hill, New York.

McKerrow P. (1988) *Performance Measurement of Computer Systems*. Addison Wesley, London.

Markus M.L. (1984) *Systems in Organisations*. Pitman, London.

Mintzberg H. (1973) *The Nature of Managerial Work*. Harper and Row, New York.

Mumford H. (1971) *Systems Design for People*. National Computing Centre, Manchester.

Poppel H. (1982) Who needs the office of the future? *Harvard Business Review*, November–December.

Pyre R., Heath L. & Bates J. (1986) *Profiting from Office Automation*. Department of Trade and Industry Publications, London.

Rowe C. (1987) Introducing a sales order processing system: the importance of human, organisational and ergonomic factors. *Behaviour and Information*

Technology, **6**(4), 455–65.

Rowe C. (1990) *People and Chips: The Human Implications of Information Technology*, 2nd edn. Blackwell, Oxford.

Sampson A. (1973) *The Sovereign State*. Hodder and Stoughton, London.

Sorge A., Hartman G., Warner M. & Nicholas I. (1983) *Microelectronics and Manpower in Manufacturing: Applications of Computer Numerical Control in Great Britain and West Germany.* Gower Press, Aldershot.

Strassman P.A. (1985) *Information Payoff: The Transformation of Work in the Electronic Office*. Free Press, New York.

Taylor F.W. (1911) *The Principles of Scientific Management*. Harper, New York.

Wall T.D. & Lischeron J.A. (1977) *Worker Participation: A Critique of the Literature and Some Fresh Evidence*. McGraw Hill, London.

Winfield I.J. (1984) *People and Business*. Heinemann, London.

Winfield I.J. (1986) *Human Resources and Computing*. Heinemann, London.

Woodward J. (1958) *Management and Technology*. HMSO, London.

Wroe B. (1985) Towards the successful design and implementation of computer based management information systems in small companies. In *People and Computers: Designing for Usability* (Ed. by M.D. Harrison & A.F. Monk). Cambridge University Press, Cambridge.

Chapter 3
The impact on organisational structure

3.1 OVERVIEW

In this chapter we look at the effects computerisation is having on both manufacturing units and other businesses. Similarities and differences are examined, with particular reference being made to the increased level of integration and control that computerisation brings. Computer information systems in organisations bring changes in either increased centralisation or decentralisation of power and changes in types of control. Empirical studies of this process in action are evaluated. The chapter concludes by looking at research into the design of the information system function itself in complex organisations. Trends are analysed.

3.2 INTRODUCTION

It is always both informative and entertaining to rehearse some of the phrases in popular usage concerning the effects computers are having on organisations. You will find that they are quite alarmist yet at the same time they seem to contain a grain of truth. Here are a sample: 'The factory of the future is going to be a ghost enterprise, the only people in it will be the odd boss and a handfull of cleaners'. 'Large office blocks and head offices will become a thing of the past, the new organisation and business enterprise will be based on remote office working, everybody will be in constant electronic communication with one another.' 'Information is the life-blood of the organisation, he or she who controls it has power.'

Everyone knows intuitively that organisations are in a constant flux of readily observable change; we are bombarded daily by the mass media with stories of takeover battles, shrinkage, expansion, reorganisation, restructuring. We know too that within organisations change takes place equally dramatically, but is usually accompanied by less media attention. Whole occupational groups disappear almost overnight (where for instance have visual inspectors gone, or draughtsmen, or key punch personnel disappeared to?). Whole departments shrink and the locus of decision-making shifts with alarming rapidity. To chart these changes, above all, to try to establish some coherent pattern to such changes is an exhilarating task for the textbook writer. Like the war correspondent or the political journalist in the front line of a war, one is aware of writing about history in the making. Serious academic studies there are, large-scale expensive case studies there are too, but things are happening so fast that today's published survey may already be out of date.

So does this mean that we cannot discern trends, begin to talk of coherent patterns, established 'laws' of behaviour in organisations? We can, but we must proceed with a large measure of caution. 'Truths' or established laws of organisational life are true only until they outlive their useful lives. Just the same as laws in science. They remain true until proven otherwise. What we have to do, then, is to be ever more critical and discerning in our information sources. The research methodology of surveys has to be evaluated carefully, asking questions such as: are the numbers sufficiently large to permit extrapolation? Or, are there special features to the survey which might render it applicable only in limited circumstances? We must not be snobbish in our sources of information too. 'Quality' newspapers, television and radio are alive to reporting history as it is happening, and on the whole they do it very well. In the field of organisations and information technology the media simplifies issues, as it must do, but at least it seems not to trivialise overmuch. In this chapter we shall selectively use such sources. In our favour is the established fact that whilst technology and products change phenomenally rapidly, organisational change does not. At least the lumbering beasts of organisations are relatively slow moving enough for us to fix them firmly in our sights.

3.3 THE EFFECTS OF ADVANCED MANUFACTURING TECHNOLOLGY ON STRUCTURE

Advanced manufacturing technology (AMT) is implemented due to specific strategic choices: these are usually (but not always) the desire for lower direct labour costs, faster response times, greater accuracy in manufacture and faster product cycle times. The vision the layperson has of AMT is of large factory units peopled by robots. The automated

Fosters lager canning plant in Australia, supplying the whole of Australasia and beyond, is 'manned' by only half a dozen personnel. It is however often overlooked that the large factory, automated or not, is not the normal state of manufacturing affairs – at least in the UK. Here the bulk of manufacturing industry is small to medium-sized. In the UK 70% of all components in the engineering sector are made in batches of less than 50, and computer numerical control of machine tools is but a small fraction (less than 5% of the total machine tool population).

The manufacturer is drawn towards AMT for reasons far different from what seem to be generally expected. The naive and outdated expectation seems to be that business wishes to rid itself of that perennially troublesome and ever-increasingly expensive element called labour. It is not difficult to see why. Robots don't strike, don't take tea breaks, don't question orders and they will work round the clock for months on end for only a squirt of grease. The manufacturer is drawn towards AMT, even if relatively small production runs are involved, because of the promises it holds out for a wide range of things. Essentially it promises greatly improved product quality and manufacturing accuracy; it promises enhanced reproducibility of products to meet specifications; it promises increased machine utilisation, reduced manufacturing lead times, reduced needs for carrying large inventories and stock levels and a markedly quicker response to new product designs (often incorporating CAD). Manufacturers are pushed to AMT and CAD by the fact that product life-cycles are shortening: the consumer is becoming ever more discerning, and by the realisation that the competitive edge is often gained through product innovation. Just how information technology changes business strategy is reviewed in chapter 6. Last but by no means least, forthcoming new legislation in the field of manufacturer liability will inevitably hasten the move to greater accuracy (hence computerisation) in manufacture.

What AMT offers to the thousands of batch producers is the possibility of a form of work organisation that approaches that of continuous process control. Nor should we underestimate the speed at which manufacturers are changing to microelectronics-based production. A survey in the UK undertaken by the Policy Studies Institute (1988) and funded by the Departments of Trade and Industry and Employment found that in the previous decade only one factory in 14 was using microelectronics in its products or production processes. By 1990 no less than two-thirds of them, accounting for five-sixths of manufacturing employment, were making some use of microchips. The effects are making themselves felt already.

Highly controlled and regularised production means that manufacturers will have to develop integrated control systems, just like other businesses are having to do, as we shall see later in the chapter. What happens is that with AMT there is a much reduced need for production managers to take weighty decisions continually on workflow control. From this it follows that the elaborate and labyrinthine management structures so prevalent in factories in the 1960s and 1970s are now rapidly becoming redundant. Supervision, control and work monitoring can now be done automatically, and high levels of manual inspection of stages of product manufacture and quality control can be drastically reduced. Attendant with this comes reduced scope for the individual manager to make what are often costly idiosyncratic judgements, especially if they are wrong! Humans are fallible and often unreliable. In this respect manufacturing units may well supply the prototype for other businesses.

Dawson and McLoughlin (1988) supply a fine case example of what happens to a whole occupational stratum of supervision. In British Rail the implementation of information technology integrated what were previously segmented control structures. The new technology obviated the need for a whole level of management hierarchy, for information about operating conditions and rail network system performance at remote locations was now immediately available on the mainframe to HQ planners and other senior management. The net result was the abolition of local or divisional control, the 'bottom line' in terms of jobs was the loss of 1000 supervisory posts. Not suprisingly, there was tremendous opposition to implementation because the loss of supervisory posts 'would have meant the destruction of a traditional element of the railway operating structure which had an important status in the organisation's culture'.

Does this change in manpower requirements mean we are going to witness a slimming of the organisational pyramid with the steady advancement of AMT? Will manufacturing organisations change their shape from the now familiar pyramid to that of the hourglass shape as legions of middle managers are rendered redundant or retrained? The consequences in terms of changes to management and supervision lead one to suspect the operation of a 'law' of the direct effects of AMT on manufacturing organisations. Does the old argument of technological determinism then hold sway here? In a survey in 1984 Child found that

	Linear	INTERACTIONS	Complex
Tight	Dams		Nuclear Plants
C			
O		AMT	
U			
P			
L	Assembly		
I	Line		
N	Production		
G	most		Polytechnics
Loose	manufacturing		Universities

Fig. 3.1. Interaction/Coupling.

most companies which engaged in batch production and had completed their computer implementation projects had experienced a greater degree of centralisation of control as a direct function of the diminished need for supervision and middle management.

Computer implementation directly affects the level of technical interdependence experienced. This leads to different parts of an organisation becoming more closely 'coupled' in the sense that Perrow (1984) means. Turbulence in one part of the organisation will therefore rapidly make itself felt in another part. Design, manufacture, stock handling, marketing and shipping all become more closely integrated – the 'knock-on effect' thus becomes more pronounced. This is illustrated in Figure 3.1.

Organisations can be linear in their interactions. By this we mean the knock-on effects are fairly predictable. A fault in one component can be traced along the chain of cause and effect. In our example a small hole in a dam will result in water seepage which will have an erosion effect and will gradually widen and deteriorate with time. Here the causal chain can be traced fairly easily. With the complex interactions in, for example, a nuclear power plant the possible causal paths at any choice point increase exponentially. There are many 'common node' functions, i.e. components are interlinked in astoundingly complex ways. The coupling is here 'tight', the failure in one can have disastrous effects fairly quickly, as Three Mile Island, Chernobyl and other nuclear accidents attest to. Factories, pre AMT, are likely to be fairly loosely coupled organisations.

There is a degree of 'slack' within the system: memos go astray, meetings are put back, people are absent. The knock-on effect to a certain effect can be attenuated and buffered by human ingenuity, by tinkering with the system, but it still rests on social content, social negotiation and slow human judgement.

As production becomes more sophisticated, as we move more towards assembly belt or continuous process manufacture, then the coupling becomes tighter. Failure in one area will quickly communicate itself elsewhere. AMT moves the organisation into the tighter coupling domain. What AMT does is drastically increase the actual amount of information processing in manufacturing units. Old systems were buffered to a large extent by the slow-moving mechanisms of raw materials handling, stock movements, paper-chasing. With the increased speed of production afforded by AMT, production itself can be tied to the immediate needs of the marketplace. Interactions themselves become more complex and interdependent. Stability of the organisation may therefore decrease not increase. The turbulence experienced will be directly linked to the marketplace, and marketplaces, as we are all witness to, are increasingly turbulent environments.

Malone *et al.* (1987) make some predictions as to what may happen to US manufacturing. Due to the decreased costs of coordinating with computers, markets and not traditional heirarchies will coordinate economic activity. Electronic interconnection will create what will become essentially electronic markets. Electronic brokerage, such as we are witness to in the international money markets, will make its presence felt everywhere. This point we have noted already in chapter 1. By electronically connecting many different buyers and suppliers through a central database, three things follow. First we are instantly able to see displayed a larger number of alternatives, second there will be an increase in the quality of alternatives eventually selected and third the actual costs of the selection process will rapidly diminish. What this means in practice for business is that as unit costs of co-ordination become lower this will result in an increased proportion of economic activity coordinated by markets. Manufacturing businesses can quite easily increase the proportion of components from other vendors contained in their products since search, selection and order placement costs are becoming so low.

Given these relationships does this give even more fuel to the technological determinism argument? Are there any particular matchings of organisational structure and operating technology? Child (1987) puts the point quite unequivocally: 'The significance of matching a particular form of organisation to the technical situation has been considerably overstated'. In point of fact a whole range of viable alternatives are available. Child concludes that there is no coherent theory of relationship between the two, with the one exception being the obvious relationship between level of automation or capital intensity and certain employment ratios. 'Sociotechnical and Quality of Working Life studies all point to the fact that there is more than one form of work organisation that could be an economically viable accompaniment to a given technology.' Real conceptual confusion exists here, Child argues, for the lack of a real relationship is due to a diversity of conceptual and operational definitions. For instance the word 'technology' has in the past covered an especially wide range of often disparate technologies and production systems.

Although we may argue over definitions, AMT continues to grow apace. We can see in the detailed case histories of implementation that strong local forces dictate how implementation actually proceeds, and with it the changed shape of the organisation. For an example of how strong local political issues (labour relations) shape the change to AMT within one manufacturing organisation (British Leyland) see Willman and Winch (1985). From the growing body of case studies, researchers and academics are beginning to formulate models of what is happening. The danger lies in attempting to apply them slavishly, in expecting every instance to fit the mould. Summarising research in both the UK and Europe, Noble (1979) concludes:

> 'Technology is not an autonomous process impinging on human affairs from 'outside' but is itself the product of social choices. Technology does not develop in a curvelinear fashion; rather there are choices, social choices, ideology, social position, the reality of shop floor struggle between the classes.'

When we look at differing forms of manufacturing we can discern that there are different organisational designs according to production contingencies. Two major sets of variables exist in relation to organisational design and AMT. First there is variabilty in quantity of production (large or small), next there is the level of product variability itself (high variability or low variability). The resultant $2+2$ matrix can yield prescriptions for organisational design. This is illustrated in Figure 3.2.

Large-volume plants producing products of low variability can comfort-

LEVEL OF PRODUCT VARIABILITY

		LOW		HIGH
---	---	Type	Organisational design	Type	Organisational design
QUANTITY OF TOTAL PRODUCTS	**LARGE**	Dedicated production plant and systems. (oil refineries) (mass production)	Mechanistic organisation High level of functional differentiation. Centralised formal planning and co-ordination	CAD with CAM equipment able to manufacture quantities of similar items (clothing manufacturer large runs)	Range of central functional departments, *but* design, production planning and control. Decentralized cross-functional teams or product groups.
	SMALL	Conventional machinery, (specialist parts manufacturer)	Semi skilled labour. Simple hierarchical structure, centralised planning by manager or group. First time supervisors handle shopfloor issues	Flexible manufacturing centres and CNC makers (jobbing engineering)	Flexible organisation. Close integration between marketing, design and manufacture. Decentralised production planning and operational control. Role integration

Fig. 3.2 Production Contingencies for appropriate new manufacturing technology and organisational design (after Child 1987).

ably have fairly mechanistic organisation structures, centralised planning and co-ordination. If the quantity of products is smaller in number and still has low levels of product variability then the organisation can be of the simple hierarchy type. There would be much 'on the spot' solving of production problems by workers and managers together.

If however we have a large-volume production plant with relatively high levels of product variability then centralised departments can function well so long as there is a degree of decentralisation of certain critical functions. These would be functions where it is imperative to be able to make decisions quickly and unhindered by elaborate administrative machinery. Examples would be the day-to-day running of production or design. Small volumes of production still with high product variability would see an organisation characterised by the close integration of roles. Marketing could work in close liaison with production (for example specifications could be changed at short notice) and design would be an integral part of manufacture.

The attraction of such a scheme of things is because it seems self-evident. But even here we must proceed with caution, because strong cultural factors are at work shaping organisations. Perhaps the best illustration of these factors at work lies in the much acclaimed survey undertaken by Sorge *et al.* (1983). German kitchen manufacturers set out to capture the quality end of the market in the late 1970s and early 1980s. The advent of AMT led the German craftsman to adapt his traditional woodworking and cabinet making skills to incorporate AMT production. He acquired a working knowledge of programming, and with it new cutting and wood forming production technology. Here new production technology was not perceived as a threat to traditional jobs, but instead it was seen as an opportunity to enlarge and extend traditional valued craft-based skills. The German example also betrays the fact that it pays the state to invest heavily in basic education for the worker.

Due to longer education and training as well as to an education system that lauded technical education basic craftsmen could rapidly upgrade their skills and become computerate. The position in the UK was (and unfortunately still is) different. Vested interests and a shopfloor system that divorces production, craft and assembly skills from 'white-collar' management take their sad toll. Computer skills are seen as basically 'white collar' and hence strictly the preserve of management. The class system prevails, and as a consequence the UK has lost the world lead in quality fitted kitchen furniture that they once had. There are important conclusions to draw from this example concerning job design which we will explore in the following chapter, but certain conclusions concerning organisational design follow from it too.

3.4 THE CHALLENGE OF CROSS-FUNCTIONAL INTEGRATION

What are the organisational constraints, apart from an archaic industrial relations policy, that precludes an organisation adapting to new production technologies? Child (1987) notes the difficulties UK enterprises face in devising new innovative management structures to house the new manufacturing technologies. The proliferation of white-collared managerial manpower (with the result that UK firms have total costs some 15–40% higher than their European counterparts) is clearly part of the problem. Elaborate management structures themselves will always create problems of work flow. Lead times become over long, and elaborate command chains and communication links will all contribute to the possibility of data becoming corrupted. Child offers a few simple recommendations to help achieve crucial cross-functional integration: the deliberate creation of special liaison roles (the post should deliberately cut across conventional management lines); attempts to integrate labyrinthine status hierarchies into neater, shorter structures (ad hoc matrix structures supply the analogue here); roles traditionally seen as separate should be collapsed and finally people should be encouraged to take on boundary-overlapping roles.

Successful companies who integrated CAD and CAM managed to link the various functions better; they promoted role convergence and allowed and encouraged people to widen their repertoire of usable skills. The result was a workforce able to demonstrate a comprehensive skill base and able to be retrained and developed. As we shall see this has implications for job design; in particular jobs become 'enlarged', people take on additional tasks and there might well be intensification of labour because of the increased control element provided by computerisation. The ramifications for the enterprise in terms of staff selection and training are therefore large. Employees who are open-minded in their approaches to learning and to what their jobs may actually consist of are to be valued and rewarded accordingly. In this respect the larger, more mature industries saddled with notorious labour relations histories are disadvantaged. As the Willman and Winch (1985) study of the UK automobile industry showed, the larger firm often experienced great resistance to role convergence simply because of entrenched and rigid departmental structures. Political resistance is forthcoming too from trade union and employee representatives, but detailed analysis of this is beyond the scope of this book.

3.5 SERVICE INDUSTRIES AND OTHER BUSINESSES

Information technology provides modern businesses with new and often radical strategic options. Because of this some writers refer to a 'crisis' facing management. In order to understand better the challenge facing business managers we need to catalogue the developments in technology and the kinds of applications that will probably result in change. Boddy and Buchanan (1988) summarise the developments in technology likely to affect business under five headings; similarly applications are reduced to five. This is illustrated in Figure 3.3.

Developments in technology should be fairly self-evident to us, it is sufficient at this stage to draw attention to the prevalence of the integrating function in both manufacturing and information services.

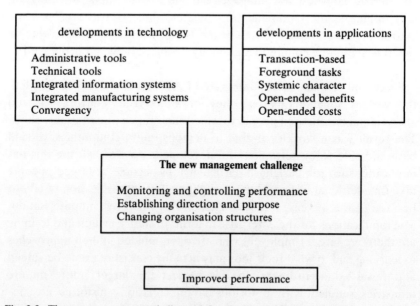

developments in technology	developments in applications
Administrative tools Technical tools Integrated information systems Integrated manufacturing systems Convergency	Transaction-based Foreground tasks Systemic character Open-ended benefits Open-ended costs

The new management challenge

Monitoring and controlling performance
Establishing direction and purpose
Changing organisation structures

Improved performance

Fig. 3.3. The new management challenge (after Boddy and Buchanan 1988).

Convergence is a phenomenon noted already – manufacturers can link CAD with CAM relatively simply. Developments in applications do present the management of businesses with particular challenges. Simultaneously with developments in technology come the challenges thrown up by the ever widening developments in applications. Transaction-based developments are those where data is captured at the original transation between client and the business organisation, for example in banks or in hotels. The management challenge here lies in using the vast amounts of immediately available information to create better profits and products more in line with market demands. The provision of much of present-day financial, travel or hotel information is now crucially dependent on the computer. Information processing is now not a backroom activity undertaken by specialist boffins, but is instead a public 'upfront' or foreground task.

Applications have their effects in a systematic way, for the influence of the microcomputer in business often spreads far beyond, say, the host department. CNC has well documented effects in tightening up planning, tooling, even maintenance functions within the factory. The effects of office systems likewise are far-reaching. Benefits, one hopes, are open-ended: efficiency should flow like new life-blood through the organisation. Often though it does not: costs are hidden, there are innumerable unforseen expenses and often there is a shortfall from the promised or expected. From Figure 3.3 we see that these two elements converge to form the new management challenge. Managers must first understand the nature of change in monitoring and controlling perform-ance. The choice here is often between decisions to decentralise or to continue to exert bureaucratic control. Challenge comes too in realising that managers usually habitually think in terms of authority lines and in vertical information flows. In point of fact the strategic use of technology forces them to relate to people differently – often across functional or departmental lines.

Boddy and Buchanan provide a useful checklist for the manager who must consider whether the organisational structure is 'up to' the demands placed on it by computerisation. First they suggest that organisational changes should be considered simultaneously when technical changes are being planned. All too often firms get themselves in trouble by doing it the other way round. Second, resources must be analysed. For example is there to be local or central provision of facilities? Who is going to control them? Third, in the light of change should any of the support funtions be reorganised? Fourth, considering both market forces and technical factors, has the right mix of local and central control been achieved? Last, but not least, there must be full consideration of those most likely to be affected by change – the long-suffering supervisors.

There has been a trend towards simpler, neater management structures in business with the advent of computerisation. The late 1960s and 1970s saw the burgeoning of elaborate management systems, the elongation of management hierarchies and the birth of fancy, elaborate multi-dimensional management organisations. But the parallel organisation or the collateral organisation and the various forms of organisational overlay (of which the matrix type is the most familiar) obviously fulfilled a real need at the time. Without a clearly identified need (rather like the world's religions), they would never have been invented.

Information technology affects the control element within business. Control is made easier because, among other things, work is automated, made faster and more efficient. That it is made easier to monitor has already been demonstrated by our comments on EFTPOS terminals. There is reduced scope for subjective, possibly erroneous judgement, and the vastly increased processing power serves easily to unify control systems that were previously scattered geographically or segmented (as in retailing satellites). Because work output is more easily monitored and measured, the porosity between work and non-work diminishes. Previously people were more or less paid by attendance. Time spent in the business organisation could easily be spent on non-work activities, engaged in non-productive labour. Let us not dodge the uncomfortable issues: the human ingenuity that goes into avoiding work or feigning work deserves a book in its own right. Since output is now much easier to monitor, people are increasingly being paid for what they produce. Contracted work is becoming more prevalent, payment by results becoming the norm. Information technology allows management up-to-the-minute data on what each worker is worth to the organisation. He or she is valued for what they can 'put through the till'.

Manufacturing, particularly if many components of the finished artefact are manufactured outside the assembly plant (as in motor manufacture), can adopt what is known as JIT or 'just in time' methods. Here parts are brought in as and when they are ready for assembly. This feat of organisation would have been too costly if not impossible to undertake in pre-microchip days. As a result firms need now carry far less bulky stock (particularly so in the field of retailing). Buying in can be more directly coupled to needs, reducing the need for costly storage space. Since stocks can be kept lower, deliveries need to be faster and more frequent – one of the contributing factors to the 16% growth in UK lorry and light goods vehicle traffic per annum.

All of these factors encourage tighter control structures, with associated simplification. Here is Child (1984) on this issue:

'As the integrations between functional activities are made more visible through integrated control systems and shared data services, so the logic of team working and networking emerges as the 'natural' basis of organisation, rather than the patterns of work and communication defined predominantly by departmental boundaries.'

We see here one of the basic contradictions that computerisation exposes in organisational life – automation of work by the microchip actually increases not decreases our reliance upon the human element. Our dependency on humans becomes more subtle, and the organisation has to take note of the fact that it is the human, negotiated order which keeps the wheels of business turning just as much (if not more) than do the inanimate parts.

A fine example of this subtle process comes from the study undertaken in the Driver Vehicle Licensing Centre (Heller *et al.* 1985). The new centre, heavily committed to information technology, used traditional O and M methods for determining the content of jobs. As a consequence the resultant jobs were narrow based and tedious in the extreme. For example, there was one job for opening the mail, another job for examining the contents, one for editing, one for coding forms and another job for applying batch numbers and so forth, right through to final dispatch of the licence. Each person, locked into closely-monitored work tasks, had no clear overview of the total system. Worst of all they were hopelessly untrained to handle telephone complaints or errors as they occurred within the system. Delays of months in processing applications let the department gain nationwide (if not worldwide) notoriety. At the heart was the fact that creating routine, boring jobs (even though they were computer-based) did not help the workers handle the all-too-frequent exeptional cases needing a degree of oversight and human ingenuity. The structural and job redesign answer was to create teams of workers in small groups who were able to give support to fellow members and other teams in times of stress. Following on from this structural reorganisation was the integration of separate tasks (requiring retraining) as well as some adjustment to the technological support.

3.6 THE DECLINE OF MIDDLE MANAGEMENT STRUCTURES

In businesses we are witnessing the weakening of vertical segmentation. Structural barriers of the vertical kind are likely to weaken because fewer and fewer people are needed to undertake functions now done by computers. In an interesting review of new technology and developments in management functions Child (1984) concludes:

'The integration of control information, its ready access by top management, and the availability of powerful analytical models renders redundant the roles of consolidating, interpreting, and passing on information which formed a significant part of many middle management and some staff specialist jobs.'

Below strategic level then the computer will make its presence felt by removing jobs. As we have seen in the case studies in chapter 1 actual job loss may be more talked about than experienced – the reality is likely to be changed job specifications. Organisations are the products of their particular histories and the business experiences of the 1970s resulted in particular structures. In the 1970s business boomed and organisations grew apace. Not surprisingly, information flow and control emerged as a pressing management problem. People in positions of power and influence, because of organisational size, began to know less and less about the whole. What was the response to this dilemma? The response was to innovate with the design and shape of organisational structures. It was the decade of the matrix, the special task force, the ad-hoc group, the temporary grouping. Mintzberg (1979) calls it by the inelegant title of the 'adhocracy'. What these temporary 'organisations within organisations' were doing was trying to cope with an increasingly turbulent environment by legitimising the informal structures that had spontaneously developed to meet a particular need. The rapid innovative informal response thus contrasted sharply with the slow, lumbering bureaucratic response which was the organisational norm of the day. To express what happened in today's language, changed methods of organising work were 'user-driven'. People urgently needed changed structures, and what the formal organisation failed to deliver was instead fabricated by the informal network.

Traditional organisation theory was, up until only recently, not too adept at articulating such needs – they were referred to vaguely and somewhat darkly as the 'informal organisation's needs'. Managers were, of course, made aware of the informal organisation by attending management education and training courses and by countless articles and books, but the usual advice was to steer well clear of such things, make only limited use of them and only then where the objectives could be precisely specified (like using them to obtain snippets of information not readily available through normal channels). Invariably they were told they were unplanned (hence they were suspect and difficult to control). Zand, writing in 1974, captures well the bottom-up drive for new types of organisational structures:

'The manager's confusion is sometimes compounded by laboratory methods and organisational development programmes. Sensitivity training, grid laboratories, and variations of group methods focus on improving the manager's skill in individual and group behaviour, but rarely introduce relevant organisation theory. When a manager applies his new knowledge to his formal organisation, he usually encourages open questioning of goals and methods, which blurs formal boundaries between jobs. Other managers interpret his actions as undermining authority and disrupting the formal organisation, so they resist and discard his changes. The manager is in a theoretical limbo; without concepts, he cannot explain what he is doing in terms they can understand.'

Business management structures then had to change.

3.7 ENTER THE NEW MANAGER

Businesses must respond to the times and the business contexts, we are constantly being told, are changing rapidly. The ability to be flexible, to adapt, to anticipate future trends and markets are qualities much admired both in individuals and organisations alike. Clearly organisations want personnel who will fit in with the future organisational shape and anticipated business climate. But if the future is unknown, what sort of animal are we after? Organisations will have to respond quickly and imaginatively to future problems: that much is certain. Zand (1974) argues that technology and the rapid pace of change in business generally will force organisations to address themselves directly to 'problems', rather than hoping they will go away or be amenable to some pre-formed bureaucratic solution. As we have already noted, the changed emphasis towards the hegemony of the market is one of the consequences of the spread of business information technology.

Organisations can be seen as divided into two basic types: we can have an organisation that is based more or less on authority, while getting the goods out come what may. Alternatively we can have organisations that are more concerned with solving the problem at all costs. Now the type of problem that each of these two types of organisations meet can itself be divided into two: well-structured or ill-structured problems. This is illustrated in Figure 3.4.

TYPE OF ORGANISATION

	Authority/Production	Knowledge/Problem
	I	**II**
Well-structured	High output Rapid processing Small number of errors in output Members low in authority report low satisfaction Tends to reject unsolicited innovations	Lower output Slower processing More errors in output More satisfying Accepts unsolicited innovations
	IV	**III**
Ill-Structured	Lower output Slower processing Lower-quality solutions Low in creativity Orderly, but not functional	High output Rapid processing High-quality solutions High creativity Appears disorderly but is functional

TYPE OF PROBLEM

Fig. 3.4. Relationship between Type of Problem and Type of Organisation (after Zand 1974).

To be swift-moving the organisation should not be hindered by slow vertical barriers to progress; structures need be no more restricting than minimally required to allow people to do their jobs effectively. Change comes fastest of all when all channels are open amongst people. Managers, decision-makers and specialists of all kinds should be able to communicate freely with one another. The organisation itself should encourage people to question goals, to query paths, to ask where the organisation is going and how it is going to get there. If a problem arises the manager should be able to enlist the help of willing problem-solvers, irrespective of who they are and in what department they happen to be located. This seems on the face of it to decribe a pretty exhilarating organisation where, if we are not careful, too much time will be spent in questioning first principles and not enough 'real' work will be done! As the service sector grows, increasingly the organisation is based on knowledge and problem-solving.

Computerisation allows the organisation to handle information better, and processing power allows tighter management control because faster response times to queries mean more on-the-spot problem-solving. If everything can theoretically happen in manufacturing on the shop floor or in service industries at the origin of the problem, then the 1970s' response of innovation in organisational design could be abandoned. If information technology once more puts management in tight control, whither the shape of future organisations? This issue brings us to confront the argument that still rages about whether or not business information technology results in a more centralised or in a more decentralised organisation. The issue was touched on briefly in chapter 1 in the context of the impact on monitoring and control systems. Now we shall consider the larger, essentially political implications for organisational power.

3.8 CENTRALISATION VERSUS DECENTRALISATION: THE ISSUES

Too much of too little quality has been written on the issue of computers and centralisation or decentralisation of power and the resultant organisational shape. It is easy to see why. Information is power. We are talking here about the the politics of who controls whom, and what it is they actually control. There are optimists around who write about the imminent revolution within organisations: dispersed processing power, 'a micro on every manager's desk' will, they predict, give a great opportunity for advancing the cause of democracy within organisations. Their arguments are engagingly simple. Devolved, dispersed decision-making within organisations will in theory bring everyone nearer strategic decision-making. Others argue that the opportunities afforded by centralised processing power will lead to tighter control structures, the outcome will be more power to the strategic decision-makers at the top. So what exactly is happening? Too little commentary has been based on real empirical studies. It is easy to see why. Empirical case studies take both time and money and longitudinal studies, perhaps the most creditable of all studies in this field, are the most expensive of all.

Early studies of the effects of computers on businesses made the sensible assumption that management desire for rationalisation and lower costs fuelled the decision to implement. It was envisaged that the success of the system could be measured simply by the improvements in the quality of decision-making. Robey (1981) however sums up more recent opinion thus:

'Recent work questions these 'rationalist' assumptions and examines the political motives behind systems development. Interestingly, rationalist perspectives tend to focus on changes in formal structure, interpreting them as appropriate moves towards greater efficiency in resource allocation. Studies using a political interpretation of MIS introduction often report that computing produces no change and favours the status quo. The protection or strengthening of existing power bases is frequently offered to explain findings of no change.'

So it seems that the optimists were naive in their youthful dreams of radical change: it is to be 'business as usual', moreover business power structures are to remain essentially the same as before. The general intention to remove vertical and horizontal barriers to management control can thus be seen as simply necessary in order to render the system more responsive to strategic requirements. Attendant with this comes, as we have witnessed, greater management control over the delivery of work. Subcontracting will increase as well as the close metering of discrete tasks or projects. In other words, control will be made considerably easier by defining and measuring outputs. Whether the organisation is changed for better or for worse for the people populating it depends on management choice.

3.9 STUDIES OF COMPUTER INFORMATION SYSTEMS AND MANAGEMENT CONTROL

We are witness here to yet another engaging paradox of information technology and it is this: computers allow processing power on the spot. But decentralisation is accompanied by increased formalisation of rules and procedures for actual job behaviour. What appears as decentralisation is in working reality greater administrative control. Now our use of the word 'control' itself has to be rigorously defined. Various writers on organisations have (as is usual in the social sciences) defined 'control' in entertainingly different ways (usually to suit their own theoretical stance). It is useful to review these here briefly. Tannenbaum, writing in 1968, defines it thus: 'control is the sum of interpersonal influence relations in an organisation'. Galbraith (1973) saw control as a 'problem of information flow', while Perrow (1972) saw control essentially as a phenomenon of cybernetics: control was about testing reality, about measuring reality and about feedback of information.

All of us are aware of the sovereignty of the market in today's sober post-industrial, post stock market crash world. Ouchi (1979) seems to take note of this for he sees within modern organisation three mechanisms of control. There is the informal social control mechanism, by which he means the organisational clans which may exist to socialise people. Next there is the bureaucratic control mechanism (through conventional line hierarchies) and finally there is the increasingly important mechanism of the market.

Markus and Bjorn-Anderson (1987) address themselves to what has become a burning issue in organisational politics and power. An everyday organisational occurrence is the burning tension between system professionals and system users. Systems people (systems analysts, system designers, computer managers and vendors) can often function as 'gatekeepers'; people have to go through them to access the system or to learn how to use it. The authors rightly note that such professionals have become powerful players in the game of organisational politics, and they exercise their power by a number of means. First their power is often wielded in relation to a specific project, for instance they will pontificate on the 'correct' type of hardware. They will exercise power in structural ways too, for they might well end up with formal authority over users – often fostering unhealthy dependency relationships. Finally they exert symbolic power by shaping people's desires and wants. All this points

to the fact that these people are having immense control over the organisation of work; often without them being intimately and professionally
aware of the human aspects involved.

Our interest lies in the fact that the 'desktop' revolution will make
people less directly dependent upon these people. Information processing
being devolved to the department level will mean that these technological
gatekeepers may be left without authority. Markus and Bjorn-Anderson
conclude: 'By reducing the opportunity for professionals to exert power
over users, these trends would appear over time to lead to greater user
paticipation in, and control over, the outcomes of system development
processes'. The ultimate outcome, whether the micro on every desk alters
power structures in any measurable way, remains to be seen. The
organisational set-ups of information technology departments (often
called by diverse names) have themselves been the object of empirical
study, and it is to these that we shall now turn.

3.10 CHANGE IN THE ORGANISATION OF
INFORMATION TECHNOLOGY ACTIVITIES

What exactly is happening to the way the information technology (or the
computing or the information systems) department is run? Where is it
placed, and in what direction is it moving? It is easy to see that there are
two opposing forces at work. On the one hand we are witness to the
tendancy to break up large organisations into profit-responsible units or
subdivisions. This is a process similar to the phenomenon of 'unbundling'
in the 1970s and 1980s: large (and not so large) organisations shedding
loss-making sections or satellites during a period of shake out and
economic recession. With the advent of relatively small profit centres
there is the parallel need to make the organisation's information
technology more responsible and responsive to unit or local needs. The
net result is a force for the devolution of information technology activities
away from the centre. Opposed to this is an equal and opposite force. We
have already witnessed the convergence of automation technology,
computing and communications technology (including telecommunications technology). There is then a force for a central overriding
co-ordinating mechanism: in practice a centralised overseeing information systems department.

Feeny *et al.* 1987 examined the design of the information systems function in complex organisations (the authors here mean by 'complex' those organisations which encompass multiple business units). All of the organisations studied were gigantic, with annual revenues between £400 million and £27 billion, with only one being under the £1 billion mark. Information system budgets were correspondingly large – between £13 million and £200 million. Eight were large industrial outfits, two were leisure and retailing businesses, one was financial services, one was a large local authority and the last one was a conglomerate. Of the 13 studied 10 were based in the UK, two in Europe and one in the USA. Ten out of the 13 organisations had experienced the following:

'Major changes in structure and control regimes since the beginning of the 1980s. In nine of the ten cases the same pattern was apparent: a new emphasis on business and business unit definition, usually in terms of product groupings; a clearer delineation of responsibility and authority between the centre and the business units resulting in greater operational autonomy for business units and often flatter overall organisation structures.'

We can construe information systems organisation structures as a continuum stretching from the extremes of centralisation to decentralisation. In between lie the forms of 'Business Unit', 'Business Venture' and the 'Federal' type organisation. The business unit approach lets the unit run as a business unit, charging for its services. Business venture means it must obtain significant revenue for itself by selling inside and outside the organisation. The federal approach is distributed, each unit controls its own budget yet it reports to central corporate management. The federal arrangement was most common at the time of the survey, having changed within the space of four short years from the previous business unit/business venture arrangement. The pure centralised form of information systems structure is fast disappearing. The author note:

'Looking ahead the Federal structure looks to be the most stable as well as the most common form in our sample. It can be adapted to align well with most forms of multidivisional structuring of the host organisation.'

What do empirical studies of the influence of information technology on total organisational structure and power tell us? Robey's 1981 survey is one of the pioneering surveys of the effects and it is often quoted as a key paper. The project involved international collaboration between research teams in Austria, Denmark, the UK, West Germany and the USA. Two major issues were focussed upon. First was there a causal link between BIT and centralisation of control of decision-making? Second, did BIT affect the horizontal segmentation of the organisation and links between departments? In only three of the eight organisations studied were there any computer-related changes in centralisation, leading the author to conclude that this is in itself an argument against technological determinism. The case examples are informative too. For example a mail order company studied experienced decentralised control over its operations. It succeeded in lowering the level of decision-making without causing top management to lose overall strategic power. Similarly a glass-making company in the UK implemented a sales monitoring system which centralised power because it 'allows top managers to review sales performance through automated reports rather than by personal supervision'.

Strong evidence was found for computers being associated with greater horizontal differentiation and with structural elaboration; in the UK the glass-making company witnessed the marketing managers actually growing in power and status, whilst the mail order company allowed informal contacts on the workfloor to solve on-the-spot problems instead of going through the authority system of the formal section head. These all point to change: how it is managed and how it is turned to overall business objectives is reviewed in chapter 6.

In conclusion Robey notes that the information technology was designed to achieve some rational objective, be it more effective use of resources or manpower or provision of a better service to customers. The technology itself did not cause any structural changes. It all seems to turn on the political context of implementation: if the organisation wishes the new technology to result in greater central control then it will see to it that it does so. If on the other hand the powers that be desire to see greater local control, then that will be the outcome. Human choice is there to be exercised. Computer technology should therefore be seen as a moderating variable – it is placed there to support either centralisation or decentralisation. Organisation theory has long abandoned the quest for the 'right' structure. It was Lawrence and Lorsch (1967) who suggested that the effective organisational form varies according to the change and complexity in the technologies, markets and environments in which it is based.

3.11 BIT AND FUTURE ORGANISATIONAL CHANGE

It is imperative to put into perspective the role of computers within the total activity of organisational decision-making. To see the brains of managers as being usurped by the computer is naive in the extreme; likewise it is naive to expect there to be radical changes in the distribution of power and control within business. Business is the instrument of the capitalist mode of production and this, more or less, goes unchallenged in the West.

Generally speaking information systems do not play a central role in the business decision-making of the main actors in business. Information technology is opening up new business areas and the decision whether to use information technology or not can be centred on whether a company wants to be in these areas. This is typically true of sectors where business is crucially dependent on technology: banking, financial services and insurance to name a few. In other sectors less dependent on computers they may play an increasing role true, but as yet the main work of management there is undertaken face-to-face, dealing with people, solving problems. Mintzberg (1973) informs us that the formal quanti-fiable analysis of business problems remains but a minor aspect of the work situation of managers. Habit, rule of thumb and generally muddling through seem the managers' norm. Only 22% of a manager's time is spent at the desktop (with or without a microcomputer on it), for he so often is working not with hard data but with 'soft' data, by which is meant information about the organisational environment and people's hopes and fears, and is dealing with their idiosyncracies. Mintzberg's original analyses seem to have survived replication even in today's micro-saturated organisational environment (see for example Kurke & Aldrich 1983). This same point is made again rather eloquently by Keen (1981) who states: 'The point is not that managers are stupid or information systems irrelevant, but that decision making is multi-faceted, emotive, conservative, and only partially cognitive'.

A rationalist model of decision-making sees all problems as amen-able to solution by computer power. The 'technological fix' will solve everything. But as we now know 'better' information in itself solves nothing; for often in organisations the result is 'information overload': people buried under computer printouts and a vastly compounded problem. To throw money and hardware unthinkingly at a problem is always lousy management style. The relativist position on the other hand sees problem solving in organisations as only remotely approximating the rationalist ideal. Here is Keen again:

'Human information processing tends to be simple, experiental, non-analytic and on the whole fairly effective. Formalised information systems are thus often seen as threatening and un-needed. They are an intrusion into the world of the users who see these unfamiliar and nonrelevant techniques as a criticism of themselves.'

But by and large we are still operating with the dominant paradigm of positivism in business at present. The unpredictable must be eliminated at all costs.

3.12 CONCLUSION

This chapter has analysed structural changes in organisations and reviewed the mixed results that surveys give us. It is up to management to see that information technology is a mediating variable in organisation life. The use to which it is put is squarely in the field of management choice, though here much turns on the degree to which the business is dependent on hardware in the first place. Shifts in the locus of power within the actual organising of information technology in organisations have been noted and the federal arrangement seems to be winning through. Finally a note of caution has been sounded. The average manager, if she or he exists, is found to be working with people's ideas and feelings much of the time. It might be a long time before computers can replace or radically restructure people who are working this way.

3.13 REFERENCES

Boddy D. & Buchanan D. (1988) The New Management Challenge: information systems for improved performance. In *The New Management Challenge: Information Systems for Improved Performance* (Ed. by D. Boddy, J. McCalman & D.A. Buchanan). Croom Helm, London.

Child J. (1984) New Technology and developments in management organisation. *OMEGA*, **12**(3), 211–23.

Child J. (1987) Organisations designed for advanced manufacturing technology. In *The Human Side of Advanced Manufacturing Technology* (Ed. by T.D. Wall, L.W. Clegg & N.J. Kemp). Francis Pinter, London.

Dawson D. & McLoughlin I. (1988) Organisation choice in the redesign of supervisory systems. In *The New Management Challenge: Information Systems for Improved Performance* (Ed. by D. Boddy, J.M. McCalman & D.A. Buchanan). Croom Helm, London.

Feeney D.F., Edwards B.R. & Earl M.J. (1987) Complex organisations and the information systems function. A research study. *Oxford Institute of Information Management. Research paper RDP 87/7.* Templeton College, Oxford.

Galbraith J. (1973) *Designing Complex Organisations.* Addison Wesley, London.

Heller, F., Karapin R.S. & Accuna E. (1985) *How Technology Affects the Quality of Employment Part 2 Case Study evidence and Example.* Sussex University Institute of Manpower Studies.

Keen P.G.W. (1981) Information systems and organisational change. *Communications of the Association for Computing Machinery,* **21**(1), 24–33.

Kurke L. & Aldrich H.E. (1983) Note – Mintzberg was right. *Management Science,* **29**(8), August.

Lawrence P.R. & Lorsch J.W. (1967) *Organisation and Environment.* Harvard Business School, Harvard.

Malone T.W., Yates J. & Benjamin R.J. (1987) Electronic markets and electronic hierarchies. *Communications of Association for Computing Machinery,* **30**(6), 484–504.

Markus M.L. & Bjorn-Anderson N. (1987) Power over users: its exercise by system professionals. *Communications of the Association for Computing Machinery* **21**(1), 24–33.

Mintzberg H. (1973) *The Nature of Managerial Work.* Harper and Row, New York.

Mintzberg H. (1979) *The Structuring of Organisations.* Prentice Hall, Englewood.

Noble A.F. (1979) Social choice in machine design: the case study of automatically controlled machine tools. In *Case Studies on the Labour Process* (Ed. by A. Zimbalist). Monthly Review Press, London.

Ouchi W.G. (1979) A conceptual framework for the design of organisational control mechanisms. *Management Science,* **25**(9), 833–49.

Perrow C. (1972) *Complex Organisations: A Critical Essay.* Scott Foresman, Illinois.

Perrow C. (1984) *Normal Accidents: Living With High Risk Technologies.* Basic Books, New York.

Policy Studies Institute (1988) *Impact of Microelectronics.* Policy Studies Institute, London.

Robey D. (1981) Computer information systems and organisation structure. *Communications of the Association for Computing Machinery,* **24**(10), 679–87.

Sorge A., Hartman G., Warner M. & Nicholas I. (1983) *Microelectronics and Manpower in Manufacturing: Applications of Computer Numerical Control in Great Britain and West Germany.* Gower Press, Aldershot.

Tannenbaum A. (1968) *Control in Organisations.* McGraw Hill, London.

Wall T.D. & Kemp N.J. (1987) The nature and implications of advanced manufacturing technology. In *The Human Side of Advanced Manufacturing Technology* (Ed. by T.D. Wall, C.W. Clegg & N.J. Kemp). Francis Pinter,

London.

Whisler T.L. (1970) *The Impact of Computers on Organisations*. Praeger, New York.

Willman P. & Winch G. (1985) *Innovation and Management Control*. Cambridge University Press, Cambridge.

Zand D.E. (1974) Collateral organisation. A new change strategy. *Journal of Applied Behavioural Science*, **10**(1), 63–89.

Chapter 4
Information technology and job des

4.1 OVERVIEW

There is evidence that while the task performance of jobs has been affected by information technology, the actual management of the task has not. The implications for this are discussed. In jobs created by technology it seems that the systems analyst has, up till now, had a large say in job design. Certain consequences follow from this. Alternative ways of designing jobs are considered, including sociotechnical systems design. The chapter concludes by looking at the new emphasis on group working brought about by recent product developments.

4.2 INTRODUCTION

It was the philosopher Ivan Illich who coined the famous phrase 'the car stands at the centre of the neurosis of the modern age'. In the light of the controversy surrounding computerisation and changed working practices, I should like to amend it to 'changing job design stands at the centre of the neurosis of the modern age'. Why should this be so? We are nothing less than haunted by fear of job loss and by anxieties about human skills being transferred into the computer and hence away forever from their human originators. We have a sneaking suspicion too, that the argument that computers will liberate us once and for all from humdrum daily drudgery is yet just another marketing con-trick, for it is plain for all to see that humdrum, boring jobs are still with us and are likely to remain so for the forseeable future. Researchers looking at repetitive VDU work and attempting to humanize the work often despair: despite attempts to give the worker greater control over the task, they have the suspicion that the job lacks any semblance of intrinsic reward and inherent meaning anyway.

The notion of doing worthwhile and basically satisfying work lies deep in our collective Western psyches. If we did not have something called work to do, then we would have to invent it: witness the physical and mental drudgery involved in a lot of so-called recreation, sport and edifying exercise regimes. To people under- or mis-employed their free time becomes the focus of their real effort, and the focus of their genuine challenging work. In practice then what is it that they do in their non-work time? They save their real ingenuity and intelligence, their real learning capacity till after work and pit it instead at entirely self-created goals. An upsurge in 'activity holidays' (surrogate work) provides people with the missing crucial challenge and meaning in their lives. The quest for meaning and adventure in out-of-work activities is, some would argue, a sad reflection of an increasingly alienated and soulless workaday existence experienced by the mass of mankind. Henry Thoreau, observing the effects of early 19th century industrialisation, had words that ring true today: 'The mass of men lead lives of quiet desperation'. Although it is mentioned but little in contemporary media discourse, job design is the culprit. It has a lot to answer for.

The weekend flight from the rat race, the eagerly awaited home time, the retreat into drugs or alcoholic oblivion, all these bear witness to the increased sense of sharp boundaries that modern work gives us. Modern work, especially computer-mediated work, is more regimented and more tightly controlled than ever before. It is more easily measured and monitored, and one is increasingly paid only for what one does. Soulless but well paid work deserves, even needs, its counterpart in hard, brute physical activity in order to purge the work-bruised psyche. To stay ahead in the modern business organisation increasingly populated by people with sharp tongues and even sharper elbows, one must be physically and mentally agile, in tip-top shape.

If but 1% of the intelligence, ingenuity and wit we reserved for our so-called 'recreational activities' was directed instead to work-specific ends, the problems of industrial regeneration and balance of payments would be solved overnight. But this ignores the political reality in which contemporary work is performed. The mass of people have to sell their labour on the labour market. They work for someone else, most likely an organisation buying their labour for what is in effect the cheapest possible going rate. If this is the reality then why give oneself totally to work, they ask? Why arrive home completely exhausted? Surely it makes more sense to keep some energy for one's own consumption; reserve some aspect of one's true self for loved ones, family and friends – for people, in short, who are beyond the reach of the crude cash-nexus.

However, most of us do not perform such equations with our lives. To pit one's wits, to use one's talents to the full, to be productive at work is seen as nothing short of Godly, noble and uplifting. All this, it may be said, is but a legacy of the Protestant work ethic. It is solely industry and work which will raise us above the level of the lowly animals and serpents: sloth and idle hands make work for the devil. But herein lies the real fear: the post industrial leisure society seems to be shaping up already. It is a society of structural unemployment and disturbingly sharp social divisions, and looking set to go more that way too. It is a society divided between those who are computer-literate and those who are not. Unemployment, marginalisation and social anomie are the lot of those without current marketable skills to offer on the labour market. Are the so-called lucky ones in employment going to gain satisfaction through using their skills? Is there going to be work left to do which engages their intelligence? Are they going to be allowed, in the face of the ubiquitous business computer, to enjoy the noble pleasures of truly creative work?

Questions posed in this way are, of course, nothing new. The advance of production technology in the 19th century provoked all sorts of outcries and warnings. Putting our contemporary fears in some sort of historical context seems to allow a little much needed distance from them. If it is known that they have been around for a long time then our worst nightmares seem just that little less morbid. Here for instance is Ure writing as early as 1835: 'When capital enlists science in her service, the refractory hand of labour will always be taught docility'. For a readable account of the history of technology-led deskilling see Rosenbrock (1984).

But is the rather depressing scenario of inevitable deskilling and mind-deadening sterile jobs absolutely inevitable in our society? We shall now selectively review some case studies of jobs and what has been happening to them over the recent years. Our focus will be on what it means to do the job, the subjective feelings associated with the job, the changing nature of tasks within the job and the duties performed. We find that whilst not all jobs are being radically transformed by information technology, there remain few that are unaffected in some way. We single out three categories of jobs for closer scrutiny: managerial jobs, the work of accountants and the work of blue-collar manual workers.

4.3 MANAGEMENT JOBS

As we have noted already computerisation brings dramatic developments in the convergence and integration of organisational functions. For example order processing, product design, production scheduling and stock control can be consolidated into one machine. The facilitation of monitoring and surveillance undermines the need for traditional supervisory positions within the management structure.

Anderson and Pederson (1980) studied a variety of businesses with up to 50 employees and with turnovers of up to $5 million. After computerisation managers reported fewer opportunities for personal contacts. Instead there were more formal meetings with more written reports and rules surrounding the job. They found that the strategic planners gained more direct control over their activities. Managers found themselves giving fewer orders and less personal advice though, as if to compensate for this, they seemed to have more appeal to influential people within the organisation. New channels of communication seemed to open up too:

'The discretion of managers concerned with control in a corporate function was fettered as a result of formal planning, which also produced a reduction in slack resources and buffer stock held and caused a higher degree of formalisation.'

Tighter coupling here leads to more formal (but more efficient) communication.

4.4 ACCOUNTING JOBS

Management accounting jobs were just as radically affected. In a review by Cowton (1987), it was found that the micro made cheap and easy the previously expensive budgetary control function. Cheap software incorporating spreadsheets allowed even small companies to produce budgets and variances easily, quickly and cheaply. Sensitivity analysis became an easy matter and budgeting itself became a routine iterative process. Cowton argues that management accounting itself is disappearing as a distinct role: it is instead being subsumed within a broader management information system. Within organisations and corporate life competition for power is rife, and there is already an emergent band of professional information specialists eager for the mantle of power.

In this respect the history of the power struggle for control of the organisation's financial information is interesting in its own right. Electronic data processing in the 1970s was conducted by big mainframes. Often these were located in separate departments and organisational power, not unnaturally, came to be concentrated there. Accounting functions were kept separate, with accountants trying desperately to keep the 'craft' ethos alive. Separation, it is argued, cost management accountants dearly as power and influence inevitably moved rapidly elsewhere.

Groups who lost power as it shifted towards the persons who developed and controlled computerised information systems have regained much of it recently with the emergence of on-line systems and the universal spread of the desktop micro. Accountants as a professional body are now much more computer-literate, thanks to the farsightedness of their professional bodies, but ultimately to the hard work of educators and trainers.

The threat to the role of management accountants as information holders continues, for with the advent of networking for instance, line managers can easily call up their own information needs. However accountants are professionally trained to use money as a unit of measurement, whilst technical and other management staff often tend to use other, often esoteric measures. The accountant thus now has a broader, communicative role, perhaps as general internal consultant on all financial matters. The proliferation of the microcomputer then forces accountants to be better communicators and to be much better at crossing discipline boundaries. Micros render accountants not less human-dependent but more so, since they are now much more closely locked into the social, linguistic and communicative realities of organisational life. They just have to interact more. In relation to job design it seems that interactive skills, social and communicative skills, are increasingly at a premium. Gone forever is the simple, narrow cognitive skill of spreadsheet deciphering and totting up the bottom line.

The implications for the design of jobs are now becoming clearer. The social component must be acknowledged and not seen as something marginal to the central role of the accountant. Chatting and socialising, counselling and meaningful communication are not time wasting, rather they can be construed as important components of organisational life. Educationalists are quick to see these changes in job demands. Social and communicative skills are now part of the curriculum for training. Selection criteria will also be affected, and so too will company policy towards staff development.

4.5 BLUE-COLLAR JOBS AND TECHNOLOGICAL CHANGE

What are types of change is blue-collar production work undergoing as a function of technological progress? In a longitudinal study of 31 workers transferred from traditional mass assembly to computer-automated batch production (CAB), Majchrzak and Cotton (1988) note six specific job changes. Not all are present in each changed job, but the points certainly have implications for job design.

(1) First came the obvious, but often overlooked, drastically reduced need for gross physical labour so characteristic of mass assembly work. (Jobs could easily be designed or adapted to suit handicapped workers here.)

(2) In the transfer from mass to CAB production a reduced sense of personal control over the work process was experienced. (This element can be taken care of in new job design by involving the operative in compensating activities, perhaps in maintenance duties or overseeing work flow.)

(3) There was an increase in the unpredictability or variability of the production process as more and smaller batches were produced. For example, assembly workers who once performed work on a large number of the same parts now performed many different operations on smaller numbers of different parts.

(4) Congruent with the need for more frequent set-ups of machines came closer social contact with supervisors and maintenance staff. Much closer co-ordination with others was required – again we see the need for careful employee selection and to reinforce and actively develop prosocial behaviour and attitudes.

(5) Because of almost continuous re-routing of work between machines (a feature of the flexibility created by CAB) workers tended to be not as closely and mechanistically locked into the workflow as they were when undertaking jobs in the old system. Workers who just wanted to stay in one place and daydream the working day away were a bad proposition for the company and were simply screened out at the selection stage.

(6) Workers reported an increase in the amount of informal communication associated with increased co-ordination duties. Human skills again appear in demand.

The authors suggest that each person has a profile of individual differences and qualities; these are what a person sees as their own unique abilities and values that they bring with them to the job. If there is a mismatch between the dimensions of the job and what the person sees themselves as possesing, then there is a poor person-job fit. Low morale, poor output and job dissatisfaction will ensue. It therefore behoves the organisation, wherever possible, to bring about a better fit by redesigning the job removing or attenuating the offending features.

Kemp and Clegg (1987) utilized the Hackman and Oldham (1975) job characteristics scale (analysed more fully later in this chapter). They looked at the degree of autonomy, skill variety, task identity and significance and feedback operations of machine operatives' jobs which were computer controlled. Some of the findings were contrary to what one would expect from the doomwatchers and prophets of technology-led deskilling. For a start operators successfully collaborated with programmers on the shop floor. In direct contrast to the deskilling hypothesis they became flexible and multiskilled and came to possess wider decision-making rights. Ninety-one per cent of operatives answered 'a great deal' and 'quite a lot' to questions about increased responsibility at work (a factor identified as having a positive effect on job motivation) and on perceived task significance. There was plenty of opportunity to utilize their skills and the changed jobs had ample variety, feedback and identity, together with lots of freedom to choose their work method. On the negative side, nobody stated that they received recognition for good work or experienced enhanced prospects for promotion – similar to the findings for typists who changed from manual typewriting to wordprocessing. What a pity then that organisation and management thinking had not caught up with the machine-led revolution in jobs. Management stands indicted.

All these findings point to the same thing: tasks change, but the political context, the organisational culture of the enterprise remains firmly in the same sad old mould. What became particularly apparent in the Kemp and Clegg study was dissatisfaction with extrinsic factors and the lack of co-operation between different functions. Only 39% were satisfied with supervision and management, whilst a substantial number of operatives expressed the need for greater participation in operational decision-making. This, one may speculate, was in order to try and use their new found experience as CNC operators in planning and co-ordinating their work. It remains an indictment of UK industry and management that the opportunities were not forthcoming for them – the class-bound nature of UK industry firmly precluded this. CNC operators were in point of fact taking a large amount of day-to-day operating decisions. They established for themselves an ethos of self-control. Indirect staff (programmers) were used, not as experts but merely as support staff. Sensitive issues of workers' control were thus raised. Kemp and Clegg state: 'It was also clear that the skilled CNC men were a powerful, largely self-controlling group and that their managers had little direct control of the production process'.

I have witnessed this phenomenon many times in UK industry during implementation. It calls for special efforts and innovative management practice. New respect, the attribution of more intelligence by management to workers, the delegation of responsibility – all will never be achieved overnight. The implications for job design remain enormous. Decisions on the day-to-day running of the highly unpredictable manufacturing unit of tomorrow might have to be taken at what for some people is seen as dangerously near to the shopfloor. Too near the shopfloor for some crusty old traditionalists. Jobs therefore cry out for sympathetic sociotechnical systems design and for all categories of personnel to be treated as mature decision-makers capable of responsibility and personal growth.

Future developments of CNC are an area of considerable speculation. Integrated manufacturing systems will increasingly be able to gather shopfloor information automatically for process control purposes. Production controllers will therefore be under even greater threat than they are already. The tasks of the CNC operator might change with the developments in technology. Job complexity might decrease, with obvious impacts on job satisfaction. The battlelines are already drawn: shopfloor control is a threat to management's right to manage, and any moves toward decentralisation would be automatically seen as potentially dangerous.

4.6 JOB DESIGN IN PRACTICE

What can we say generally about the design of jobs once they have been affected by information technology? Clearly the potential for creating interesting, stimulating jobs and to look afresh at the meaning of jobs is with us now, perhaps more so than ever before in history. The critical issue in job design here is the point at which the computer is to take over from the human. What element of the job is to be left to the human? How is it to be done? Federico *et al.* (1980) put the issue quite succinctly: 'What needs to be established is the point at which the computer should replace man, the point at which it should assist him, and the point at which it should not be used.'

If genuine opportunity exists here to think things afresh then many commentators argue that a golden opportunity has been scandalously thrown away. Typical of such thinkers are Wall *et al.* (1984), who conclude that despite the challenges offered by new technology the oldest, most tired solutions to the problems of job design have been unthinkingly adopted. In their article entitled 'New technology, old jobs' they conclude their review of four illustrative case studies with the following:

'Our overall message is simple. Technology, whether new or traditional, has a major impact on task performance but less on task management, i.e. on the control of decision-making rights over the day-to-day management of work. Much previous work suggests that this latter factor is a critical determinant of the quality of working life for shopfloor employees. Achieving a balance of control over work depends to a large extent on the strategic choices exercised by management.'

The sensitive management of technology-led change must be one of the goals of the 1990s. To throw at a new problem old solutions will not be sufficient anymore. Education and insight, knowledge and nous are what management needs.

People, then, are doing different tasks often requiring a different emphasis on skills, but the power contexts in which they are doing these remain the same. Despite opportunities things remain unchanged. Traditionally technology comes first. Work design is seen as a later, non-essential development; to a certain extent it has even been perceived as something of a luxury. Implementation is seen as an unproblematic activity, as simply a mechanical process governed by strict Taylorist principles. Let us now look at what ought to be the case.

4.7 JOB DESIGN: THE TERRAIN OF THE SYSTEMS ANALYST

The installation of the first wave of business information technology was fuelled by the desire for lower labour costs. Taylorist and rationalist principles held sway. It was the era of the systems professionals; above all else it was the era of the systems analyst. However systems professionals were not trained in analysing human needs. They often made wrong assumptions (many of them woefully wrong) about human needs. Checkland (1984) remains the most trenchant critic of systems theorists and their pervasive influence upon job design. Their dominant paradigm of existing methodology is a positivistic one. It is a mechanical, 'nuts and bolts' approach to people and jobs. Above all else the unpredictable must be eliminated in any system. Systems are therefore made foolproof simply by reducing the need for expensive skilled labour. Systems are improved by making them independent of human intervention since (so they argue) humans are inherently messy, unpredictable and fallible. The best system is one that is self-contained, self-diagnosing, self-regulating and self-learning. If only business functioned cybernetically, like a well-tuned thermostatically controlled central heating system, all would be well. It exists in the minds of analysts as some kind of Platonic ideal – glimpsed but dimly, but always striven for.

What were the results of jobs designed by systems professionals? They were inevitably jobs that were tightly defined, with the emphasis more likely than not on close, often stifling, supervision. The classic case must here be the DVLC example examined in chapter 2. Here there was a close breakdown of jobs akin to an old-style moving assembly belt. The only difference was that there were substantial amounts of new technology mixed in. Appalling job design led to low output, low involvement, low motivation and singular lack of commitment. That this state of affairs continued for so long is interesting, for it represents the power of a particular dominant ideology. Computers have here become not simply an enabling technology, they have instead constituted an actual defining technology; they force us to see problems in particular ways, they force us to define existence itself in particular ways. Zuboff (1988) even goes so far as to maintain that it is becoming increasingly difficult, if not impossible, to define ourselves in any other way. Such is the power of dominant technology.

The relationship of systems analysts to job design becomes more understandable if we consider that traditional accounting practices and costing systems rarely show up the shortcomings brought about by neglecting human factors. Let us not underestimate the scale of the disaster (for that is what it amounts to). To illustrate this, the use of information technology and subsequent job design in the Inland Revenue, the Social Security system, the National Health Service, the UK Civil Service and sections of private industry was severely criticised by the public sector Comptroller and Auditor General. Willcock Mason (1987) said of a 1984 report prepared by the Department of Trade and Industry in conjunction with the Institute of Administrative Management: 'The information bill of companies was $5 billion per annum and rising. Of this an estimated 20% was wasted expenditure'. Companies it seemed had hoped to cut their workforces by work rationalisation. Instead the net gains were often zero.

So what were the premises of systems thinkers who designed such poor jobs (and in many cases still continue to do so)? Their notion of the enterprise was that the reality experienced by us all was somehow a simple consensus. All problems, human or otherwise, were reduced to problems of co-ordination and regulation. Conflict was seen as a deviation from the expected norm, for systems thinkers had absolutely no time for messy human perceptions or shortcomings. But it is worth pursuing this issue further here, because this approach is in itself a poor application of systems thinking. True to form, systems analysts consider the economic and technical system of the enterprise in which the job is placed – this much one would expect. But they then go on to ignore the wider social, human, environmental and political system in which it all takes place. Systems thinking should describe the total system; anything else is shortsightedness. For this oversight systems thinkers can be hoisted by their own petard.

Patently what is required is a systems methodology that is sensitive to human vagaries and needs. One such so-called 'soft' systems methodology is the Checkland methodology (Checkland 1984). Traditional methodology and 'soft' systems methodology are compared in Figure 4.1. Sections 1 and 2 of the soft systems methodology have already been advocated in chapter 2: a closer, finer-grained analysis of what it really means to work in organisations, together with a close study of how people really work and what will give them true work satisfaction. This approach, which avoids descriptions of people in terms of inputs and outputs, is what soft systems methodology is really about. The radical approach comes with eliciting the support of users in job and system design, a point to which we now turn.

4.8 SOCIOTECHNICAL SYSTEMS AND JOB DESIGN

There is extant a large literature, complete with prescriptions for action, for sociotechnical systems implementation (see for example Butera and

'TRADITIONAL' SYSTEMS METHODOLOGY	'SOFT' SYSTEMS METHODOLOGY
1. Problem definition	1 Data collection (quantitative and qualitative) a) What is the situation? b) What are people's perceptions of the problems in this situation? c) Are attitudes considered?
2. Choice of objectives	2. Situation analysis a) rich pictures of situation (see fig 2.1) b) identify issues in the situation c) identify primary tasks and essential activities d) establish relevant systems from b) and c)
3. Systems analysis a) data collection b) fact recording c) analysis of recorded facts	3. Root definition precise description in words of relevant systems
4. Generation of possible solutions	4. Conceptual model model of activities which relevant systems logically perform
5. Selection of best design solution in the light of financial constraints	5. Compare abstract model with rich picture and reality a) does the logical model happen in real life? Why not? b) construct agenda of possible changes
6. Client approval	6. Debate possible changes with client, problem-owners and problem-solvers a) What is systemically desirable? b) What is culturally feasible?
7. Systems design output, input files, processes, controls, program design and testing	7. Implementation of agreed changes
8. Implementation	

(between items 2 and 4 in the left column, marginal annotation: is it logical? *)*

Fig. 4.1. 'Traditional' and 'soft' systems methodology compared (after Willocks and Mason 1987).

Thurman 1984). Both the soft systems approach and the attendant sociotechnical approach have a particular model of man as a basis. This model asserts that people possess to a larger or smaller degree a set of needs which must somehow be satisfied by the work process and it is up to sensitive systems design to do something to achieve this. For example, Emery (1978) cites six human needs which he claims should be borne in mind in any sociotechnical systems design endeavour:

(1) The need for the content of the job to be reasonably demanding – demanding, that is, in terms other than demanding sheer endurance or staying power.
(2) The need for people to learn, develop and grow on the job and to be able to carry on doing so.
(3) The need for a degree of social support and for the proper recognition of effort.
(4) The need for a certain amount of decision-making which the individual can exert.
(5) The need to be able to relate what is done at work and what is produced to the person's own social life. Work should have inherent meaning and confer human dignity, not degrade people.
(6) The need for the worker to feel that the job leads to some form of describable future.

Noble sentiments all, but what is their real working value to the work planner? The trouble with theories of human need is that catalogues abound. Each theorist construes his or her own set of needs; and documented needs have proliferated by the thousand. Are human needs as perceived by sociotechnical systems theorists therefore of any use to anybody? To put it even more bluntly, what exactly do they mean? The trouble with Need Theory (for that is what they are called), is that the needs are couched in language of such vague generality they are open to any amount of interpretation.

According to one interpretation of systems theory a large proportion of people working with information technology are working with jobs that are positively psychonoxious. For example, what are we to make of the USA, where the sector which is by far the heaviest user of information technology is the military/industrial complex? Weapons and weapon delivery systems, manufacturers and arms suppliers are all part of what is cynically misnamed the 'defence industry'. Do all personnel involved in such work interpret it as degrading to the human spirit? Or are they so alienated from their real selves that they cannot see and describe their true predicament?

The participative approach to job design is the very cornerstone of sociotechnical systems design. To demonstrate its importance in an age of acronyms it too sports its own: ETHICS. This stands for Effective Technical and Human Implementation of Computer Based Systems, and the seven-stage approach proceeds as follows:

(1) Diagnose both the human and the social needs. If necessary issue a questionnaire in order to evaluate job satisfaction and employee needs which the new system should be designed to meet. Discuss the results with employee groups.
(2) Next specify first the social then the technical objectives, and then all technical requirements and constraints.
(3) Set out the possible technical solutions. Evaluate these against the ability to fulfil technical objectives. Next establish the possible social objectives and evaluate the ability of each to fulfil the specified social objectives.
(4) Compare the social and the technical solutions, assess the compatibility of each social solution with each technical solution. The result should be a list of genuine, achievable 'sociotechnical' solutions.
(5) Rank the sociotechnical solutions by evaluating each against the social needs and the technical objectives in stages (1) and (2).
(6) Prepare detailed work design to assess the type of jobs that will result.
(7) Accept the best possible sociotechnical solution.

Sociotechnical systems design applied to actual jobs may be a noble attempt to redress the balance in favour of humans. However, as a system it is not without its critics. First it has been criticised as being able to function only when employee numbers involved are small. Essentially it is consensus participation. Inherent in this approach is the notion that there should be a hierarchy of participation (see for instance Mumford 1983), but many people nowadays regard the establishment of elaborate status hierarchies as rather old hat and boring. But perhaps the most damaging criticism comes from those who maintain that the sociotechnical system's approach has been highjacked by conventional (i.e. Taylorist) forces existing already within the organisation. Once regarded as 'alternative', radical, a counterforce to the prevailing orthodoxy of 'machines and profit first', the sociotechnical systems approach has nowadays become attenuated and institutionalised, and poses no real threat to the prevalent Taylorist orthodoxy. That battle will unfold during the 1990s.

4.9 PERSONALITY CHARACTERISTICS

In the early days of business information technology – in the dark distant days of the large mainframes, of separate computing departments, of programmers and analysts as handsomely paid superstars – computing was an acknowledged back-room activity. And a particularly intense cognitive activity it was at that. As such, people with particular psychological profiles were attracted to it and it was they who subsequently found they could command rich rewards. Computing staff were found to be significantly lower in terms of need for social reward and peer contact than other matched occupational groups in the workforce. Their reward came not from human contact, but instead from solving difficult problems, debugging and getting programs up and running. In this respect the popular stereotype of the reclusive scientific boffin was not far from the truth, and a whole lucrative service industry grew up selecting the 'right' personnel using pencil and paper psychological tests. Job design as a consequence took a serious downturn. Human and social factors in jobs were studiously ignored, for employers blindly assumed everyone who came in through the door was uninterested in them. This damaging legacy lives on today, even though now business information technology is ubiquitous throughout the organisation and employee characteristics have themselves radically altered. Apart from closely defined specialist jobs we are unable to specify the personality and psychological parameters for many jobs. Indeed, even in job requirements in the UK computer supply industry, a recent survey indicated that only 16% of jobs in information technology actually required formal qualifications. Experience rather than qualifications is what mattered in three out of four job advertisements (Sparrow and Pettigrew 1988). Background and education appear to count for very little here. All types are welcome: if you can learn the job and produce the goods on time, the job is yours.

4.10 JOB CHARACTERISTICS AND INFORMATION TECHNOLOGY

One model of the job characteristics particularly germane to the study of information technology is that propounded by Hackman and Oldham (1975). Feelings of personal worth and job satisfaction are gained by three, what they term 'critical psychological states' (centre column of Figure 4.2). Experiencing these three states leads to distinct feelings of personal well-being with attendant positive work outcome: self motivation in work, high quality work performance and job satisfaction (right-hand column of Figure 4.2). But the critical psychological state is

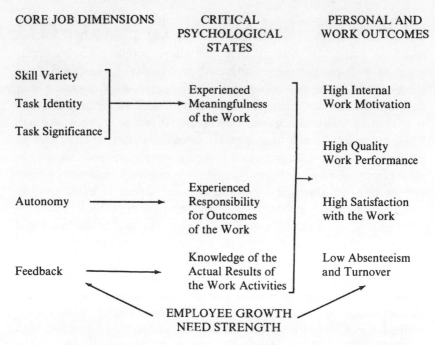

CORE JOB DIMENSIONS   CRITICAL   PERSONAL AND
                          PSYCHOLOGICAL   WORK OUTCOMES
                              STATES

Fig. 4.2. Job characteristics model of work motivation (Hackman and Oldham 1975).

derived directly from the work itself. In particular it is created by the five 'core' job dimensions (left-hand column) of skill variety, task identity, task significance, autonomy and feedback from the job itself.

These five dimensions have quite explicit definitions in the Hackman and Oldham scheme of things. Skill variety refers to the degree to which any job needs a variety of different activities, skills and talents. Task identity means the degree to which the job requires the holder to complete a whole, clearly defined unit or piece of work. Task significance is the degree to which the job has an impact (positive) on other people, be they other employees or people outside the organisation. Autonomy should give the holders feelings of freedom, permit them to use their own discretion and to be free to schedule their own work. Feedback means that job performance can be readily related to results.

From Figure 4.2 we can see that experienced meaningfulness of the work is derived from the three core job dimensions of skill variety, identity and significance, and that responsibility is derived from autonomy and knowledge of results. How do the various core job dimensions relate particularly to jobs in information technology?

4.11 TWO EMPIRICAL STUDIES OF JOB DESIGN

Of the precious few empirical studies undertaken on what happens to jobs and their motivating potential when technology takes over, the one by Kahn (1987) stands out from the rest. This was a longitudinal study of the work of travel agents – an industry transformed by the impact of information technology and still reeling from the rapidity of this change. Within a period of five years over 80% of travel agents gained access to interactive videotex and the world's largest travel and timetable databases. This is a situation not unlike the rapid acceptance witnessed in the banking, finance and retail sectors.

Using a questionnaire based on the job characteristics model of Hackman and Oldham, the author found a number of results with serious implications for future job design. First and foremost it was found that job satisfaction was directly related to the power of the facilities used. The simplest facilities elicited the lowest satisfaction; the most complex the highest.

Does this mean that people are slavish computer power junkies? Obviously the hypothesis needs to be subjected to closer empirical scrutiny, but one suggestion is that there is an inverted 'U' shaped curve expressing the relationship between the level of satisfaction and motivation and the level of technology used. Up to an optimum point users gain satisfaction, beyond that point, the point at which human ingenuity and expertise become encoded in the expert system, motivation and satisfaction seriously decline. Professionals who have their skills expropriated in this way could well become demotivated – a point only time and further research will tell. The spread of expert systems and artificial intelligence will have to be monitored closely; empirical studies of usage still appear to be at the anecdotal level.

Implications are apparent for organisational training and human resource policy too, for it was found that if staff had no previous experience with business technology and were then introduced to it within the organisation, then these people experienced greater satisfaction than those who had been previously organisationally exposed. This suggests a strong motivation to 'keep up with the Jones's' and that the retraining of existing staff rather than recruitment of 'green' labour might be both more humane and productive in the long run. I can attest to countless cases across UK industry where I have been involved in just that. People respond to upgrading, learning new technology-based skills. In terms of work relations and group size both the job demands and the hardware used seemed to dictate that smaller groups of co-workers (up to nine people) were the most satisfying work configuration. We see here the finding, replicated many times elsewhere, that technology is not necessarily leading to socially isolated work, but is instead once again placing the emphasis squarely back with the primary working group. This is a point we return to later.

In another study of job change Buchanan (1985) notes how the potential for enhanced job design was thrown away by lack of management insight into human needs at work. A firm of consulting engineers had their engineers (primarily working out in the field) write reports in longhand and then present them to the company typists. With the purchase of expensive word-processing hardware and software and subsequent implementation management suddenly became unhealthily preoccupied with control issues. The company immediately grouped the typists into two word-processing centres, taking them away from the small groups in which they had been based previously. (The typing groups had been servicing particular groups of consulting engineers.)

The avowed management aim of this change was to control the flow of work to and from the typists. Each group had a supervisor and a workflow co-ordinator. Output was six times higher, and the number of typists employed was decreased, but there were several problems with the new system. More time was spent proof reading as reports were much more easily amended. Waiting time for the engineers was not reduced as had been expected and job satisfaction for the typists was reduced due to a number of reasons. They were unhappy with the reorganisation into two centres as they now no longer knew which authors they were typing for – work was collected and strictly allocated by the supervisors. The typists did not get to know the writing style and idiosyncracies of expression of each author as before, thus making transcription from page to screen more difficult. Due to lack of personal contact they were unable to present possible formats and presentation styles on screen to the authors, thus wasting a possible advantage of the system. Queries were no longer taken to the author direct, so the typists would simply 'take a stab' at possible interpretations of handwritten text. This in itself led to more time correcting errors and reprinting.

The consulting engineers, as the authors of the documents, were themselves not made aware of the capabilities of the system, nor for that matter its constraints. They therefore made unrealistic demands on the system and grossly underused its potential. In all it seemed that no one was really satisfied with their job under the new system – the authors lost the ability to liaise with the typists and the typists themselves were suddenly subjected to stiflingly close supervision and to social distancing from the authors whom they respected.

This is an example of the organisation of work frustrating the effective complementarity of human and technical skills. Management was just trying to control the work too tightly; if they had left the typists with the author groups (but still located in a pool) they would have solved all the above problems. They could have had the advantage of sharing expensive equipment, close cover for holidays and illness and all the other advantages of social support. As it was many of our respected core job dimensions – meaningfulness, a direct link with work outcome, knowledge of results – were callously destroyed. The social system had instead been torn apart and cobbled together round a framework provided by the technical system.

4.12 DERIVING JOB DESIGN FROM WORKER DEMANDS

So how exactly should we generate the detail of job design? We can be guided by the general concepts of sociotechnical systems design, but thinking nowadays seems to have moved on towards specifying detailed cognitive and social needs. This is a point made clear by Clegg (1984). From a review of the available literature it appears that the UK is falling behind in specifying closely job design and new technology. In this respect the mainland of Europe is way ahead. Illustrative of this are the detailed specifications drawn up by Schardt (1986). Taking clerical tasks as an example the author notes that the actual design of the software will so often dictate what the job actually consists of: the demands, rewards and challenges encountered in daily tasks. In many respects clerical work involving word processing software and database manipulation constitutes a useful paradigm for other jobs transformed by information technology. The German Trades Union Federation drew up suggested guidelines for four interfaces: the input/output, dialogue, tool and monitoring interfaces.

In terms of dialogue interface the German Institute for Standardisation (DIN) has already specified certain minimum criteria for dialogue design in terms of the following: reliability, fault tolerance, transparency (the ability of the software to explain lucidly) and controllability by the user.

All the recommendations seem sound enough, governed as they are by the need to reduce operator stress. The sad fact is that so much software in current use in offices signally fails to meet these worthy criteria. If the standards bureaucrats had their way much of current working software that people spend their lives toiling with would be relegated to the dustbin. The recommendations, they argue, are based on accurately surveyed worker demands and because of this they deserve our closest scrutiny:

(1) The dialogue should always be under control of the user.

(2) It should be possible to individualise the dialogue. The argument is that individual styles of operation (within acceptable latitudes) are more attractive than standardised formats. The report suggests such moves are conducive to self-realisation in work. In reality however the results are already with us, for software is on the market that is sensitive to, and adapts to, the level of sophistication of the user.

(3) The goal should be an optimum mental workload with plenty of variety in tasks and performance.

(4) Fault tolerance should be inbuilt.

(5) Demands for criteria regulating the tool interface include the workers being able to manage their local data source and being able to progress with the task at their own local workstation. Here it is envisaged they will be able to produce small 'individualised' applications proceedures. In respect of the provision for the local modification of standard applications software, the market is already catching up with user demands. In all, the continental demands for work orientated criteria for software seem light years ahead of the usual narrow functional and financial criteria in current use. This becomes even more apparent when we consider the thorny issue of the division of labour between person and machine. Psychosocial factors such as operator underload or operator overload should be countenanced as well as the possibility of job enlargement and job enrichment.

(6) Finally for every job there should be the provision of minimum task contents for that part of the job left assigned to humans.

In the last respect it is interesting to compare how close these standards come to the following Hackman and Oldham empirically–derived core dimensions:

- There should be minimum levels of variety; for example no single task such as word-processing should be done all day.
- Wherever possible, tasks should be holistic in nature, with a sense of achievement for the completed task and a sense of closure or finish at the end. Satisfaction comes from seeing part of the job 'in the can' and seeing the job completed and well done.
- There should be psychologically complete tasks: different components of a complete task, namely planning, disposition, performance and controllability, must be represented in the job. Satisfying tasks should not be interminable: they should have a beginning, a middle and an end.
- Provision should be made for social contact.
- Incentives for learning and self-development should be provided.

4.13 USER-CENTERED SYSTEMS DESIGN.
THE WAY FORWARD?

Might the problem of the design of systems and software be overcome simply by more exhaustive surveys of user needs, somewhat akin to the ones cited above? If the texture of work in the future looks set to be determined by the software and its limitations and vagaries, surely it is a fairly simple matter (and more inherently democratic) to design according to people's collective wishes? The attraction of an intuitively simple solution appears irresistible.

Hooper (1986) cautions us against the pitfalls involved in slavishly following fashion. He draws an analogy between user involvement in systems design and software and user involvement in architecture. Community participation in architecture he argues was a disaster, whose net results were far from perfect. Instead he claims what is needed is an interface science, with its developed principles and coherent philosophy, not unlike the Bauhaus movement in architecture. If however we look at the contribution of human factors experts in interface design we see that their contribution has been minimal.

Gardiner and Christie (1987) cite research undertaken with systems designers who were asked questions on guideline usage: 63% claimed they did not use any guidelines at all. At a human factors talk 447 designers were asked to 'write down the major steps one should go through in developing and evaluating a new computer system for end users'. Early focus on users and tasks was mentioned by only 64%. Only 40% mentioned empirical testing and only 20% mentioned iteration; only 16% mentioned all three.

The modest impact of guidelines on design must be explained. It might be that human factors guidelines are either too local or too global in scope to be of use to the practitioner 'on the shopfloor'. More likely there are organisational constraints at work; for instance the aversion of the host organisation to call in human factors experts on these issues. Guidelines do not require interpretation, whereas design principles do. In this respect human factors experts are able to recommend principles from two main areas: from the psychology of memory and from the psychology of skill acquisition. Together these constitute recommendations which have far reaching implications for work well-being and the reduction of stress. Software should make plenty of use of temporary labels and parameters (i.e. versions of current files) in order to reduce the memory load on operatives. Users often arrange their current subgoal in a hierarchical arrangement. The system can help users here by displaying visual reminders of their position if called upon to do so. How can systems be made easier to acquire? Studies of how people learn systems gives us clear principles. There are three types of psychological changes which underlie skill development: changes in knowledge, in process and in strategy. As we become more familiar with a system we change our perception of it. As we become more skilled we can bypass certain proceedures. And as we become better we can reorganise our strategy for operating the system.

There are three discernible phases to skill acquisition, according to Winfield (1989). In the early cognitive phase the learner tries to understand and perform on the system using his or her existing habits. This stage is characterised by the slavish application of verbal rules. Systems designers can therefore make life easier for the learner by giving plenty of opportunity for rehearsal of what has been learnt and by providing extensive feedback on progress. It is important that people start out on the right foot: early errors tend to persist unless corrected. In the intermediate stage of skill acquisition new patterns of skill components are tried out. People put together 'wholes' of what they have previously learnt in a piecemeal fashion. They are less reliant upon verbal rules and as such the designer can reduce the volume of feedback. In the last phase, the autonomous phase, all skill components become automatic and there is less possibility of interference from other tasks. Overt verbalisation actually slows people down at this stage. In the early stages then a well designed piece of software will use few declarative statements: the emphasis will be upon carefully controlled exploration.

4.14 DEVELOPING GROUP WORKING

The primary working group heavily committed to the use of hardware (possibly networked) is now receiving the close attention of researchers. In this respect networks and even worldwide 'metanetworks' have been catalogued by researchers (see Quarterman and Hoskins 1988). How can group working methods be made more efficient? Stefic *et al.* (1987) developed what they termed 'meeting tools': a co-ordinated interface to enhance group methods of working. Information was to be shared by all and a sense of teamwork deliberately fostered. In an 'ideas development' applications package public and private interactive 'windows' would let people share what they think. This has been done by 'windows' on information, as well as simple tools to support simultaneous action. The emphasis on group working in the future will force software developers to enhance such methods, they argue. Tools need to be developed which actively support and enhance simultaneous action by co-workers. Co-operation, not isolated competition should be the norm. The small isolated screen is set to be replaced by the large flat blackboard (or whiteboard) workscreen; the technology is not far away.

Developers of corporate workteams, sports psychologists engaged in team development all talk of synergy: the added quantum of energy that comes about when people pull together in a team. The team is more than the sum of its parts, it seems. Information technology seems set to tap this fascinating and productive concept. The question remains: is management ready?

Stefic *et al.* (1987) explore the possibility of a 'meetings spreadsheet'. The authors note that disagreements about decisions taken in meetings have primarily three causes. First people have specific property relationships with ideas, with proposals, with arguments, etc. They come to think that they own what they are voting on. Second, there have been unstated assumptions in debates and third there have been unstated criteria. (These last two are what are sometimes referred to as the 'hidden agenda' of meetings). What the authors propose is software and hardware that can upstage what even the best meetings chairman can do. To aid the group through the phases of group decision-making they propose the following:

• In the first 'proposing phase' all proposals need to be displayed to the group by a set of connected windows called, rather old-fashionedly, 'proposal forms'.

• The next phase, the 'arguing phase', calls for reasons to be written down, preferably in clear 'pros and cons' terms where participants can add statements or modify existing proposals.

• The last phase, the 'evaluation of ideas phase', is best explained by referring to it as a sort of 'argumentative spreadsheet'. Here a proposal is viewed and evaluated in relation to a specific set of beliefs. Different viewpoints are characterised by different belief sets and since these are displayed publicly for all to see all is then above board and common knowledge.

Computer-supported group work will undoubtedly come to the forefront as the decade progresses. In management tasks in particular we can see that automation is now ready to augment the essentially social nature of managerial work. For this reason in the development of social software and hardware we are witness to multidisciplinary research teams. Social psychologists and occupational psychologists work alongside ergonomists and software development specialists. (Greif 1985). Product design seems to be forging ahead. Winograd and Flores (1987) describe a computer program which analyses conversational speech acts to help workgroups communicate together:

'It is the first example of a new class of products that we are calling 'co-ordination systems' or 'workgroup systems' for use on computer– communication networks (which might be based on local networks, time sharing, or advanced telephone exchanges) to which all of the participants have access through some kind of workstations. Its objective is to make the interactions transparent – to provide a ready-to-hand tool that operates in the domain of conversations for action.'

One case study documenting the essentially social nature of changes in people's jobs after information technology was implemented is found in

Buchanan and McCalman (1988). In the study of a hotel installing a computerised booking system and software for basic clerical and administrative duties, they noted immediate positive effects. First there was a perceived heightening of confidence in management decision-making, overall financial performance became more 'up front' and publicly visible. (By these are meant room occupancy rates, unpaid bills and so on.) Managers for their part became more pressured by their own staff for rapid responses to events. In this respect, rather than wiping out the middle management role computer systems in hotels and the hospitality industry as a whole are being used as valuable support mechanisms. In an instant they remove the uncertainty previously associated with decisions based on inadequate information.

In terms of job design the lessons to be drawn from this case are legion. Staff actively wanted to know how the software functioned, particularly in terms of supplying the specific information which helped their work performance. Job design should therefore include a liberal amount of training and job enlargement. Because profit and loss became more visible and talked about, many more people became involved in the lively debate about the running of the whole show. Management had more time to concentrate on the welfare of guests, and so there became an emphasis on the social skills needs by all categories of staff.

4.15 CONCLUSION

We now know enough about the elements which make satisfying jobs: these are quite low in number, they seem on the face of it like good old-fashioned common sense and they do not cost the earth to install. Why, then, are they ignored so much? Why is it that when one listens carefully to people's grumbles about their work these usually involve the simple violation of some elementary principle like, say, feedback, job variety or recognition for due effort? It is because we are trapped by history. We are trapped in that historically the employer could simply dump the person if the job was lousy. A residue of unemployed, potentially trainable labour was there to be tapped. Lousy job design survived despite bleeding-heart liberals and concerned social scientists, as well as the organised might of the remains of the labour movement.

Now, just as jobs are becoming shaken up by technology and there is the opportunity to rethink what actually constitutes a satisfying, worthwhile job there looms on the horizon something more revolutionary than anyone could ever imagine ten or so years ago: large-scale labour shortages. Demographic changes ensure that if lousy jobs exist it is the jobs that will be changed, not the long-suffering incumbents. Staff will have to be cajoled, looked after, respected and rewarded. New labour markets (females, older workers, the disabled, ethnic minorities) will have to be courted actively. In short, labour will become more discerning in how it sells itself. The net result will be that the psychological content of jobs will become more closely examined than ever before. And none too soon!

4.16 REFERENCES

Anderson N.B. & Pederson P.H. (1980) Computer facilitated changes in management power structure. *Accounting, Organisations and Society*, **5**(2), 203–16.

Buchanan D. (1985) Using the new technology. In *The Information Technology Revolution* (Ed. by T. Forester). Blackwell, Oxford.

Buchanan D. & McCalman J. (1988) Confidence, visibility and performance: the effects of shared information in computer-aided hotel management. In *The New Management Challenge: Information Systems for Improved Performance* (Ed. by D. Boddy, J. McCalman & D. Buchanan). Croon Helm, London.

Butera F. and Thurman J.E. (1984) *Automation and Work Design*. North Holland, Amsterdam.

Checkland P. (1984) Systems theory and information systems. In *Beyond Productivity: Information Systems for Organisational Effectiveness* (Ed. by T.M. Bettelmans). International Federation for Information Processing/North Holland, Amsterdam.

Clegg C.W. (1984) The derivation of job designs. *Journal of Occupational Behaviour*, **5**, 131–46.

Cowton C.J. (1987) Management accounting and new information technology. In *Management Information Systems: The Technology Challenge* (Ed. by N. Piercy). Croom Helm, London.

Davies A. (1987) Organisational aspects of management information systems. In *Management Information Systems: The Technology Challenge* (Ed. by N. Piercy). Croom Helm, London.

Emery F.E. (1978) *The Emergence of a New Paradigm of Work*. Canberra Centre for Continuing Education.

Federico P., Brun K.E. & McCalla D.B. (1980) *Management Information Systems and Organisational Behaviour*. Praeger, New York.

Gardiner M.M. & Christie B. (Eds) (1987) *Applying Cognitive Psychology to User Interface Design*. Wiley, Chichester.

Greif I. (1985) Computer-supported work group: what are the issues? In *Office Automation Conference 1985 Digest*. World Congress Center, Atlanta, Georgia.

Hackman J.R. & Oldham G.R. (1975) Development of the Job Diagnostic Survey. *Journal of Applied Psychology*, **60**(2), 159–70.

Hooper K. (1986) Architectural design: an analogy. In *User Centred System Design* (Ed. by D.A. Norman & S.W. Draper). Lawrence Erlbaum, London.

Kahn H. (1987) New technology and job satisfaction – a case study of travel agents. In *Human Computer Interaction – Interact 87* (Ed. by H. J. Bullinger and B. Shackel). North Holland. Elsevier Science.

Kemp N.J. & Clegg C.W. (1987) Information technology and job design: a case study on computerised numerically controlled machine tool working. *Behaviour and Information Technology*, **6**(2), 109–24.

Levin M.F. (1983) Self-developed Q W L measures. *Journal of Occupational Behaviour*, **4**, 35–46.

Majchrzak A. & Cotton J. (1988) A longitudinal study of adjustment to technological change: from mass to computer-automated batch production. *Journal of Occupational Psychology*, **61**(1), 43–66.

Mumford E. (1983) *Designing Human Systems*. Manchester Business School, Manchester.

Quarterman J.S. & Hoskins J.C. (1986) Notable computer networks. *Communications of the Association for Computing Machinery*, **29**(10), 923–71.

Rosenbrock H.H. (1984) Designing automated systems: need skill be lost? In *New Technology and the Future of Work and Skills* (Ed. by P. Marstrand). Frances Pinter, London.

Schardt L.P. (1986) Integrated software design: a work orientated approach to the humanization of contemporary clerical tasks. In *The Psychology of Work and Organisation* (Ed. by G. Debus and H.W. Schroiff). North Holland. Elsevier Science.

Sparrow P.R. & Pettigrew A.M. (1988) Strategic human resource management in the UK computer supplier industry. *Journal of Occupational Psychology*, **61**(1), 7–23.

Stefic M. *et al.* (1987) Beyond the chalkboard: computer support for collaboration and problem solving in meetings. *Communications of the Association for Computing Machinery*, 30 January (1), 32–47.

Ure A. (1835) *The Philosophy of Manufactures*. Charles Knight, London.

Wall T.D., Barnes B., Clegg C.W. & Kemp N.J. (1984) New technology, old jobs. *Work and People*, **10**(2), 15–21.

Willcocks L. & Mason D. (1987) *Computerising Work: People, Systems Design and Workplace Relations*. Blackwell Scientific Publications, Oxford.

Winfield I.J. (1989) *Learning to Teach Practical Skills: A Self Instruction Guide*, 2nd edn. Kogan Page, London.

Winograd T. and Flores T. (1987) *Understanding Computers and Cognition: A New Foundation for Design*. Addison-Wesley, Massachusetts.

Zuboff S. (1988) *In the Age of the Smart Machine: The Future of Work and Power*. Heinemann, London.

Chapter 5
Computerisation and management choices

5.1 OVERVIEW

The introduction of information technology is part of the never ending cycle of change experienced in an organisation. The concern of management should lie in not simply reacting to change beyond its control, but in shaping the actual course of change. This chapter examines some of the key issues and choices facing management throughout the change process brought on by information technology.

First some of the reasons for the poor track record of management in this field are examined. What we need is an agenda for the implementation and management of new technology based upon a thorough knowledge of its effects. Second the chapter examines social inertia within organisations and the related phenomenon of counter implementation strategies. Management strategies to overcome such resistance are examined here.

The study of effective management can yield pointers to success with information technology; it can also alert us to the politics of the control of information technology. Finally, there is growing evidence that the pace of change within organisations is irrevocably speeding up. People's perceptions of the organisation, their relation to it and their relationship with other people within it are changing too. This is best understood by studying an organisation's internal culture.

5.2 COMPUTERISATION AND MANAGEMENT CHOICE

Many people spoke hopefully of the 'computer revolution' when it first came to public consciousness around the year 1978. That was the time when pundits, politicians, journalists and the chattering classes in general first harangued the ever gullible public with the term. To be more precise media attention became more focussed immediately after the transmission of the apocryphal BBC film *Now The Chips Are Down*. From that point onwards people began to talk in earnest about the very real challenges and dangers facing management.

What did they say? What were these hopes and fears expressed in those early, heady days? Once again in public parlance the word 'revolution' popped up, genie-like in everyday conversation. The spectre of revolution haunted Europe in 1917; visionaries, students and romantics spoke of revolution in Europe in 1968. Ten years passed and again revolution was on everyone's lips. This time though it was the computer 'revolution'. Of course all revolutions have their professional hangers-on, just like all wars have mercenaries who follow them, and there is evidence, on the west coast of America at least, that the revolting students of the 1960s turned their intelligence in the 1970s towards microchip technology and related product design. But concomitant with all the talk of revolution came the nascent ideas that accompany all revolutions. All revolutions, social or otherwise, force us to rethink fundamentally our social and economic relationships; they present to us opportunities for liberation, opportunities for freeing the human spirit from its humdrum bondage and offer instead scope for the unleashing of repressed creative talent. A revolution presents a schism in our way of thinking, and it gives us the opportunity suddenly to see the world in a radically different light. The momentous events in Eastern Europe in the late 1980s bear witness to this.

Simply because the word 'revolution' was bandied about all manner of radical hopes and ideas were raised, and none more so than in the area of management choice, to which we now turn.

5.3 MANAGEMENT OPPORTUNITIES

How would work become liberating? We know that robots could be made to do the dull drudgery of labour-intensive assembly work, but how for instance might the nature of managerial work be transformed? In the period of unbridled optimism that characterised the late 1970s and 1980s popular reasoning proceeded thus: computer power is cheap and getting cheaper by the month. People's outputs can now be monitored, analysed and evaluated more cheaply and more efficiently than ever before in human history. The traditional role of management was to survey and oversee output, to monitor, to cajole and to discipline the workforce. It has been argued that this will be usurped by the ubiquitous computer. Now if work outputs can be monitored and measured easily then there should be unbridled opportunities for people to earn simply by reaching their set work targets. Close surveillance and repressive man-management are just not necessary any more. Subcontracting work out, the unbundling of labyrinthine organisations, performance indicators and immediate results monitoring – all these spelt death to close managerial control and to associated long involved command structures. Put simply: if you turned out the goods, put cash through the till, added your bit to the bottom line of profitability then all was well. You were free to do whatever you pleased (more or less). Come and go as you please, work long hours or short ones, sport whatever dress took your fancy, all was fine so long as the bottom line of the printout was OK.

Dress became freer, new careers opened up, flexitime grew. The hours of work grew as people made hay while the sun shone. All this was, in its own quiet way, revolutionary. Management had been concerned in the 1950s and 1960s with socialising, cajoling, persuading, counselling and above all else understanding the work force. That was the valuable legacy of the Human Relations school. The emphasis throughout had been on specifying behaviour: specifying how to do it; specifying which rules applied and which did not.

But specifying behaviour is ultimately demeaning – demeaning both for management and workers alike. What the computer bluntly did was to specify not behaviour, but results. The computer specified goals, goals both measurable and payable. You were allowed all the freedom in the world just so long as the results looked and felt good. Just so long as that bottom line glowed profitably.

The events of the 1970s undoubtedly had profound effects upon management. Individual managers felt themselves squeezed and often unseated from their traditional roles (and more likely than not out of a job). It was the decade of the big management shake out, most of all in manufacturing. It happened not before its time too, for there were already emerging vocal critics who argued that there was just too much management in business and industry, in effect too much control, too much specificity of objectives and too much mediocre or bad management. Above all they claimed that this was what was stifling people's initiative. If commercial momentum was to be sustained people, it was argued, had to free themselves from the shackles of old ideas and control mechanisms and instead contemplate radical solutions. This radical critique of overmanagement found its eloquent spokesperson in the work of Cornuelle, whose influential book *De-Managing America: the final revolution* was published in 1975. Here is a flavour of his argument:

> 'Our reliance on management has produced a society that is less than it could be. We are collectively much less than we are individually. Management suppresses and limits, diminishes the quality and quantity of our human responses.'

and further on:

> 'Management which manages by specifying behaviour is dehumanizing and inefficient. Management which manages by specifying results is emancipatory. It opens to all the possibility of inventiveness and resourcefulness. It is a way of depoliticizing the management process.'

From our standpoint here in the 1990s were those radical, emancipatory opportunities actually created?

5.4 MANAGEMENT CHOICE, MANAGEMENT INADEQUACY

Management came late on to the information technology bandwagon. Whilst the lower-level jobs of clerks, machine operators, data input, data preparation and cost accountants were being transformed overnight, the day-to-day work of managers remained for all intents and purposes untouched by information technology. We can discern four distinct uses of the computer for decision support for management. In the first era, in the 1950s and 1960s, data processing in the payroll and accounting function were the areas affected. In the second era, during the 1960s and 1970s, the computer became extended to manufacturing, stock control and online order entry. The third era, from the 1970s onwards, witnessed the first intrusion into the strict domain of management. By this is meant information systems, decision support systems and the advent of desktop micros (possibly networked) in the manager's office. The fourth era, commencing in the middle 1980s, was witness to the growing intrusion of global communication technology, artificial intelligence and expert systems.

Top management's response to interactive computing by and large has been slow. Current surveys all show minimal use by top management of artificial intelligence and expert systems. Growing, that is for sure, but still small. Why? Senior management work is simply less open to an algorithmic solution and automatic performance than are other occupations, and from this there follow a number of ramifications which make themselves felt throughout organisational life. First (and most obviously), management knowledge about and interest in computers is, despite a few notable exeptions, pretty low. Following on from this, it follows that management's knowledge about the human and social consequences of computerisation is likewise correspondingly low. By this we mean the necessary working knowledge and confidence to handle successfully the pragmatics of implementation, how to resolve people problems, how to handle training problems, how to handle counter-implementation moves by the workforce and the myriad other issues surrounding the murky internal politics of computerisation. Whilst management's knowledge of information processing and information systems design can in certain cases be nothing short of astounding, management's handling and control of human issues is still at the age of the plough.

The response of top management to interactive computing in the late 1980s has been surveyed by Martin (1988) at the National Computer Centre, UK. As an ex computer services manager, the author of the report could be said to have inside information. In his study he found that the typical senior manager's job involves several hundred fleeting social contacts or social 'episodes' during each working day. His somewhat fragmented daily work pattern involves obtaining information principally from personal, face-to-face sources (71%), whilst only a small amount of information is gathered from impersonal sources (29%). His day typically consists of using informal sources for data gathering, using the social network of personal contacts and carefully listening to the grapevine. A heavy reliance on verbal sources of information of necessity left little time for extended, step-by-step logical and analytical thinking. Time spent absolutely alone for extended reflection or for quiet introspection was almost unheard of. Instead he was more concerned with seeking the assistance and co-operation of talented and like-minded people than with long-winded computational analysis. One study found that the typical executive was uninterrupted for a half hour or longer only nine times in all over a four-week period.

What sort of social working world does this lead to? The most common catchphrase of the harassed and stretched executive is 'time is money'. It leads, or so common opinion would have it, to an intense consciousness of the passage of time and ultimately to the disease of our modern age:

'hurry sickness' and stress. Life is seen as nothing but a battle against the chief adversary the clock, for every minute is precious and has to be used to the maximum profit-gaining advantage. It is a superficial approach to work, for of course the quality rather than the quantity of time spent should be of paramount importance.

The veneer of bustling efficiency may mask pointless, poorly planned, unproductive work; many argue that what is needed is not more hustle and bustle but serious extended reflection on where the organisation is going and why it is doing what it is. Real cost savings come from changes in the way people work and from radical rethinks. Huge savings are not necessarily made by lopping seconds off essentially trivial tasks. But the manager's and senior executive's day is perfectly adapted to the particular demands of the job. Of course it can be improved, for who cannot improve their work output in some way? But it cannot be fundamentally criticised or radically altered, say by automation or by computerisation. If the executive's life style and work style is criticised then it must be from a standpoint of a lack of real understanding of them.

The information technologist who sweeps into the office with expert systems or artificial intelligence 'answers' to the problem is profoundly misguided. In Martin's 1988 study, the reason why senior managers stopped using interactive computing facilities was engagingly simple: they could not use them because they were out of the office for most of the time. This highlights an important feature of management. Despite the enormous efforts by vendors to convince managers they will be more efficient and get more work done if only they had the latest, most expensive pager/fax machine/cellphone/laptop computer/relational database/computerised personal organiser, we now know that, odds on, they won't.

The North American business scene, apart from Japan, is the most information technology-saturated environment ever encountered on this beautiful fragile earth of ours. American productivity, market share and new product innovation have drastically fallen during the 1980s and early 1990s and look set to fall further still. People can be literally buried in the latest high-tech gadgetry yet still be doing the wrong thing. They can be ruthlessly efficient yet be hopelessly ineffective. So much work, at least in offices, earns the contemptuous epithet 'busy fools'. Radical rethinks and shake-ups require just the sort of input that our precious gadgetry is so poor at delivering: hard, clear, ruthless logic which questions fundamental business premises. At heart is the distinction between our old friend 'efficiency' and 'effectiveness'. An explanation will help. Efficiency is about doing things right. Doing it so that it looks bright, new, labour saving, slick. Effective work on the other hand is about doing the right things. Whereas the small-minded manager would be wary of costs per unit of output, his sharper business compatriot would ask if the right product was being produced in the first place. Similarly a manager can become easily inundated with the crisis or fire-fighting mentality of solving problems, but what is needed is the ability to produce creative, workable alternatives. The efficient manager will be obsessed with the performance of a given task as well as is possible in relation to some predefined, unquestioned performance criterion, again it might not be the right thing to be doing anyway. An efficiency mentality leads to defensive behaviour, to safeguarding resources; an effective orientation asks 'are we optimising resource utilisation?'. Slavishly following duties gets us nowwhere fast; the effective manager is concerned with obtaining results. Finally lowering costs should be secondary to increasing profits. The analytic approach to effectiveness and efficiency in management has been developed by Drucker (1970, 1980) and Tapscott *et al.* (1987).

Since the domain of the senior manager is not immediately threatened by the computer they must of necessity be lacking in first-hand knowledge of the threat. If they have not experienced the feelings of resistance and hostility to organisational change themselves then how can they be expected to understand and 'manage' such feelings in others? The growth in short management training courses on the practical human aspects of managing computerisation is one answer to this management crisis. For only now are we beginning to document and codify the phenomena of resistance and to devise strategies to overcome it that can readily be used by managers. First of all though, human resistance to computerisation and the choices it presents to management have to be placed within the wider context of organisational change generally.

5.5 INFORMATION SYSTEMS AND ORGANISATIONAL CHANGE

The message from chapter 3 is unequivocal: computers within organisations are mediating rather than causal variables. What this means in practice is that computers increase rather than decrease the scope for management choice. Organisation theory of the late 1960s and 1970s was concerned with large-scale all-encompassing theories. This theorising on a grand scale gave us simple prescriptions such as 'centralised structures were associated with placid environments; more differentiated ones with turbulent environments', 'small is beautiful' and so on. This led directly to our thinking in causal terms when computers arrived on the scene. Computers, it was suggested, must somehow result in large visible shifts. Shifts, for instance, towards either centralisation or decentralisation. These were the simple themes which preoccupied writers and researchers, commentators and journalists alike.

Our knowledge concerning the specific effects (after considerable empirical research) is that organisational structure is, as was known all along, caused by well-known fundamental influences such as the business and working environment, the level of technology and the size. What computers do is merely strengthen and deepen such relationships. If there is a tendency towards centralisation then computers will speed up the process; likewise if there is a tendency towards decentralisation then computers will speed that up too. Choice comes in because there can be a conscious decision by management to design an organisation's structure in a particular way. For management then, computers can be designed to fit in with existing management and organisational structures. On other occasions computers come in the wake of organisational change itself. We can see that system design and organisational design are areas of crucial decisions for management – decisions that, because of the huge capital costs involved, are often of life-or-death importance.

An information system is indelibly linked with organisational structure and it requires, on the part of management, an intimate awareness of both the technical and human aspects. The truth is that this area of management choice is so often left to technical specialists – specialists who are so often blinkered by their own narrow specialisms. Yet its importance is all too often overlooked by management. Systems design can in practice be organisational design, and there is no more predictable way of redesigning an organisation than to fundamentally change its information system. Robey (1983) demonstrates how even within a central co-ordinating system in an airline, essentially local events and management choice can steer the course of history. One airline was eager to computerise – it was quick to see the advantage of easy computer-managed decentralised organisational 'satellites' spread across the country's airports. Naive management steeped in causal reasoning may have predicted eventually a greater centralisation of structure, and with it ultimately greater bureaucratisation. What emerged in practice was that information fed in locally actually strengthened local teams and emergent local and national matrix structures. The case illustrates the development of purely local, lively organic teams. Management were quick to realise the positive morale-enhancing nature of this change to local teamworking and were smart enough to endorse it with prosocial and proactive company personnel policies. It might serve too, as an example of how a prevailing culture (a conscious expectation of tighter computer-mediated centralisation) can be overcome, shaped and changed by deliberate management choice.

5.6 OVERCOMING RESISTANCE

There exists no word better designed to strike terror into the hearts of those who are concerned with managing new technology: resistance. People experiencing any organisational change – computer related or not – show a surprising (even bewildering!) variety of behaviours. This is not surprising. The organisation comes to represent a multiplicity of things to them. To many people it will be kind, benevolent, generous, rather like a loving parent. Yet to others it will be the source of anger, frustration even despair. People will project on to the system all manner of fears and frustrations. 'This outfit will see you right – provided you don't upset the boss.' 'Nobody rises in this organisation without a large amount of creeping.' Such sayings will constitute an organisation's shaping force and will eventually become its dominant culture, as we shall examine later in the chapter.

Understanding resistance and management's response to it involves us in viewing people as being driven by forces, forces which the people are often unable fully to understand themselves or even to articulate publicly. To understand their surface behaviours we have to probe beneath public appearances and posturings. The hostility people may express at the introduction of systems is merely an expression of their felt frustration. Frustration derives from conflict and conflict, as we all know, arises because people see somewhere a threat to the satisfaction of their human needs. In workaday reality this means that people will deliberately withhold data, they might even provide unwanted data just in order to disrupt output. In other words they will display all the varieties of expressive behaviour of lowered morale in the workforce, from absenteeism through to deliberate acts of workplace sabotage.

Hirshheim and Newman (1988) note that each of the three phases of computerisation has associated with it characteristic patterns of resistance. In the systems analysis stage we might find that users are unwilling to participate in the requirements specification. So what do they do? They go absent; they cannot be found; everybody seems to have urgent dental appointments; key documents mysteriously go astray; everyone is away in crucial meetings elsewhere. In the implementation phase apathy and lack of interest can be uppermost, while in the live operation phase resistance can sometimes surface which has been lying dormant throughout the previous two phases. The sorry catalogue here includes all the age-old woes of industrial and commercial life: low productivity, poor efficiency, high labour turnover, organisational infighting, absenteeism and aggression. Hirshheim and Newman list a number of the more common causes of resistance which management could do well to heed.

(1) First the traditional 'explanation' of resistance often refers to people's innate conservatism and is the standpoint of the writer Machiavelli quoted at the opening of chapter 2. It is fatalistic and somewhat depressing for it assumes people will never change. It is a dangerous assumption, for the 'status quo' and habitual ways of behaving are there only as long as people allow them to be. Dictators both of right and left persuasion are fond of subscribing to the innate conservatism argument.

(2) People can say that they simply do not feel the need for a new system. Optimistic managers will say that this is merely because they have not been convinced or 'persuaded' of the utility of the new system. They argue that time and effort will have to be spent in 'selling' the system.

(3) If people are not actively participating in the change process they will quite naturally express lack of involvement. It is up to management to adopt enlightened participatory policies here.

(4) With computerisation, resources will almost inevitably become redistributed. Each person can ask themselves the following questions: is it possible for me to improve or defend what I have already? Can I increase my budget equipment/staff/status/ego/power/control over information/ownership of information?

(5) Any system must be seen to 'fit' the organisation's culture and if a change is required then the whole of the work force should be made

aware of the goals and be wholly committed to them. A user can perceive an information system as essentially not 'fitting' his or her own personal cognitive style. The process of matching information system design with individual personality profiles and methods of problem solving is still in its infancy (for a useful summary see Benbaset and Taylor 1978; Yaverbaum and Sherr 1986; Lansdale 1988.)

(6) The system must accord with good ergonomic principles. Ease of learning and 'friendliness' rate high.

(7) The personal characteristics and idiosyncrasies of the designer may show through in the system and therefore may be seen as unfriendly by staff. Technical staff are often unversed in user interests and needs.

(8) The organisation may suffer from a deficit of educated and trained staff. Local labour may have a strong orthodoxy against training and change.

There exists no one simple prescription that will solve every organisation's problem with resistance. Each organisation will have its own unique way of responding, and clearly what is immediately required on the part of management is a sensitivity to both the complexity of systems development and the social and political nature of associated organisational change.

5.7 STUDYING GOOD MANAGEMENT PRACTICE: THE RACE TO EDUCATE MANAGEMENT

Researchers and business writers now seem confident that the time has come for surveys to broadcast the distinguishing features between firms successful in their information technology implementation and firms less so. The profile of the successful company, according to the Kobler Unit for the Management of Information Technology (1988), can now be drawn up and this we shall now examine. For management the need for this type of research has never been higher because more and more attention is now being paid to management making mature investment decisions in information technology. The Alvey committee reported that in 1987 current UK investment in operational information technology systems was £40 billion. We have already encountered figures which suggest that an alarmingly high proportion of this is wasted expenditure.

Put bluntly, the race to educate the UK managers in information technology is now on. And on in earnest, for word is getting round fast about the poor track record we have in investment decisions where information technology is concerned. The Department of Trade and Industry in association with the Institute of Administrative Management published research findings in 1985 which, thanks to their wide circulation in both the business and popular press alike, shocked many thousands of business people out of their complacency (Kearney 1985). Thankfully here is a case where the tabloids' simplistic, attention-grabbing one-line headline did the trick admirably. 'Up to 20% of expenditure on new technology is wasted', ran the business section bold headlines. Shock tactics, gross oversimplification of results and some judicious streamlining of painstaking (and expensive) research findings worked wonderfully well. The iconoclastic news fell upon an audience of managers and business people eager for the truth about information technology. They wanted an approach to information technology that went beyond the seduction of the up-to-the-minute state of the art; that went beyond the glossy computer vendor marketing hype. The answer seemed to lie not in heavy investment in the latest most powerful hardware. Sensible investment policies based upon careful analysis of people's past mistakes came slowly to have currency in everyday management thought.

More detailed examination of the Kearney consultant's report reveals a wealth of findings directly relevant to improving management's knowledge. The research divided users of information technology in all sectors into two categories: 'advanced' users of information technology (the 'leaders'), followed by the unsophisticated users of information technology (aptly labelled the 'laggers'). Comparing company return on capital employment, the laggers were 'six times more likely to have poor financial performance in their market sector than sophisticated users'. An effective information technology strategy was what differentiated the two. We can now say unequivocally that an effective business strategy in an increasingly competitive world is made by focussing on critical issues. What information technology does is allow measurement to drive action. Companies will be greatly disappointed with their investment in the information technology field if they do not seize the opportunity it affords to rethink fundamentally both their business and their marketing strategy.

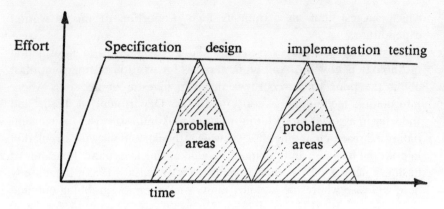

Fig. 5.1. Phases and Potential problem areas.

5.8 WHY COMPANIES FAIL: POINTERS TO SUCCESS

Each phase of implementation has its own characteristic difficulties. The specification stage and the design stage are all fraught with difficulties, moreover the overlap between stages poses particular problems, as illustrated in Figure 5.1. Here it can be seen that 'overlap' occurs where one type of thinking, language or approach interacts with another. From specification to systems analysis through to translation into systems design – all stages present genuine communication problems.

As actual implementation takes place there emerges another set of problems which stem from the dialectic between design and implementation. The problem comes when one discipline base, language and epistemology comes up against another one. Problems of semantics, understanding and interpretation thus occur in the translation effectively across cultures and life worlds. Even in literature translation, there are those who maintain the act of translation always causes loss of meaning and subtlety somewhere (Steiner 1975, 1978).

The current 'second wave' of information technology investment (as it is now known) aims above all to be more self-aware of such communication pitfalls. In the first wave the primary use of information technology was undoubtedly to cut labour costs. This can be effective in fighting short-term fires, in trying to minimise declining profits and in possibly reducing high labour costs and/or overhead costs. What research into good management practice reveals is that today the leading companies are moving away from short-term cost-cutting exercises in favour of trying to gain longer-term effectiveness. Investment in information technology should therefore be judged in terms of defence of a company's vulnerability to attack by competitors. A competitive strategy based upon information technology would consist of all of the following:

- A declared aim to improve measurably customer and client services.
- A declared aim to be more responsive to individual customer or client needs.
- Improving the time from product design to market.
- Accelerating the cash flow cycle.

The Institute of Manpower Studies conducted in 1988 an ambitious research programme involving 150 companies, each of which was a major user of information technology. The institute's report makes sobering reading. Up to two thirds of the managers contacted had no experience of information technology of any kind, and examples of good practice in the management of information technology were, to quote the report, 'few and far between'. The report becomes all the more valuable then, when the researchers conducted in-depth research into how successful companies were actually proceeding. The results are salutary.

5.9 GOOD PRACTICE: THE CHANGING ROLE OF MANAGERS

Good practice was characterised by a marked change in the nature of managerial work: the senior managers and directors concerned with the implementation of the systems had an approach which was at once 'participative, reassuring and motivating'. Their approach could be broken down into five related elements:

(1) They ensured primarily that the systems were aimed at meeting genuine user needs. They aimed at the actual identification of user needs, not through any short-cut method but instead through careful discussions with the managers concerned. It was acknowledged that the discussions were both tightly structured and long. Genuine participation does not come cheap.

(2) The keynote was participation and commitment throughout implementation. How was this achieved? Users (or their representatives) were made members of the project teams that saw the project through from

beginning to end. Managers at the beginning were not treated contemptuously as 'computer illiterates', instead they were treated as customers whose information needs had to be articulated and fulfilled through long exploratory dialogues. Again time and effort were involved.

(3) Managerial work itself would change in dramatic ways: there would be less boring and repetitive work. In turn the managers would face new personal challenges emanating from training, and with this came the possibility of personal development.

(4) Training therefore became crucial. Training was seen as one way of improving the confidence, motivation and status of managers.

(5) All the information technology-driven changes heralded changed jobs and with these changed jobs came a reformulation of what good performance should be and what the commensurate rewards should in fact be.

The case studies of successful companies revealed that the managers concerned were aiming for rapid business growth and with it possible corporate reorganisation. To ensure a necessary high degree of staff commitment and motivation there was the emphasis on what was termed the 'satisfiers'. These were job design elements not unlike the various parameters of good job design encountered already in chapter 4. The company was committed to offering interesting and challenging work, and implicit within this was the feeling that it was the staff, not the hardware, that constituted the company's most precious resource. Careers, it was felt, must offer both challenge and the opportunity for progression, and there must be a declared company aim to be able to 'offer rewards at a level commensurate with productivity, efficiency and aspirations'.

Such recommendations for management which come from studies of good practice are naturally broad-brush in approach; obviously they need to be intelligently interpreted to suit the context of each company to which they are applied. In practice, management is a battleground of competing interest groups, and when we examine what actually happens in managerial implementation programmes we are witness to some gruesome skirmishes.

5.10 KEEPING MANAGEMENT CONTROL AFTER IMPLEMENTATION

Management is driven by down-to-earth pragmatic considerations. Rarely if ever will it reason taking a 'principled' stand or proceed in its reasoning from some ideological or principled premiss. Management works from what is known; it 'flies by the seat of its pants'; it works on an incremental basis when faced with complex decision-making processes, and the no-nonsense assumptions it makes about the outcome of implementing information technology are by now well catalogued. In fact it transpires that there are only a few major categories of assumption; although management may not use the following labels for what they describe as the expected outcome, research seems to see all falling under these categories (Kling and Iacona 1984).

First, management can be besotted with the notion of 'technological evolution', for it can work with untested assumptions often based on popular or media-generated simplistic assumptions. For example it can be led by a blind faith that the system will lead the organisation towards being more integrated – and that after implementation the happy corporate family will be in constant amiable communication one with another. The reality as we have seen can be radically different. The outcome can be either a tighter or a more distributed organisational structure, depending on management choice and on the forces acting upon it. The process is only hastened by the addition of information technology.

Management can also see information technology as 'sharpening up' the whole organisation, in a modern variant of the Darwinian 'survival of the fittest'. Management may hold the belief that after the universal implementation of information technology only the most cost-effective organisations will survive.

Another interpretation of what might happen is that the new technology will merely hasten up the long known phenomenon of organisational drift. Organisational goals can, and indeed do, change over time. Those goals themselves might even conflict one with the other across time. The computer, it is argued, may simply contribute to this fragmentation.

Kling and Iacona (1984) studied organisations implementing complex inventory control systems in medium-sized manufacturing firms where the systems were shared by many divisions. They found that 'key actors' or persons who creatively furthered the goals of computerisation came to be significant forces within the organisation. Craftily they used the politics of computer-based management information systems to enhance their own power and control. It appears then that human choice becomes paramount. The bogey of technological determinism has at last been exercised. But exactly how did these influential people operate? They operated by conscious choice, by cunning ploys, by force of persuasion, by enlisting networks of support – even by enlisting Machiavellian politics. Human ingenuity (and forward thinking) become paramount.

In a sense therefore it is a misnomer to speak of the 'evolution' of an information system. An information system never does simply 'evolve' in a non-describable manner. The concept of evolution underplays the very real role of human conscious decision (even deviousness), of self-directed and cunning self-interested behaviour. So what does the effective games player know about the organisation and its life blood that sets them apart from lesser mortals? He or she appreciates that organisations are but elaborate coalitions. Systems then become the direct product of social forces, of struggles for dominance, of attempts (successful or otherwise) of sabotage, of compromise. Each different workgroup will have their own computing preferences, all of which derive from their own particular partisan approach to the work in hand. The effective gamesplayer in the implementation game will intuitively understand this. A senior level 'fixer' is therefore needed, who will be in touch with these organisational forces and who can give legitimacy to the winning coalitions.

Kling and Iacona studied in detail the politics surrounding the acquisition of a materials requisition planning system. One new system was purchased at a cost of over $430 000, more or less because manufacturing staff experienced excessive inventory problems. (A multiplicity of product lines meant that planners could not handle continuous updates.) A loose coalition emerged of the data preparation manager, the systems analyst, the production control manager and the materials control manager. Management adopted the strategic plan of presenting the system as 'socially neutral'. They consciously played down any changes that might follow from eventual implementation. Seminars were organised which were seen both as useful propaganda for the system and as 'ideological training'. Top managers encouraged employees to join a professional organisation, to go on courses and to gain eventual certification in materials requisition planning. The high-level participants (managers) in the system formed a coterie and soon developed their own jargon to the exclusion of the other groups. For example, the marketing function did not understand the powerful 'techspeak' and argot, and hence were excluded from crucial discussions. The senior level 'fixer' role came to be filled by the vice president of manufacturing who managed, not unnaturally, to get priority for manufacturing out of the new system. Simultaneously there also emerged an informal expert on micros who came to oversee development in the microcomputer fields. He was deliberately used and became assisted in his endeavours by willing senior staff.

5.11 ORGANISATIONAL CULTURE

The media-grabbing antics of high technology firms and high technology entrepreneurs have focussed people's attention onto the flavour or texture of life in these firms. Make no mistake, a firm's culture can grab your attention as soon as you walk through the door. People can be open, smiling and conversing in a free and frank manner which is both enlightening and encouraging. People speak highly of one another; they speak highly of the organisation as a whole. They feel as if the organisation is working for them; helping them achieve and grow in personal worth and stature. Such a frame of mind can for example manifest itself readily in the smile and attitude of the lowly receptionist. On the other hand, the briefest of visits can reveal negativity, backbiting, collusion, an atmosphere of recrimination and mistrust. 'If only people spent less time fighting each other and getting on with work, things would be much better' is a phrase often encountered. Many different variants of this expression abound.

A precise definition of an organisation's culture is given by Deal and Kennedy (1982): culture is 'the integrated pattern of behaviour that includes thought, speech, action and artifacts and depends on man's capacity for learning and transmitting knowledge to succeeding generations'. How does such a nebulous concept show itself in organisations? Deal and Kennedy maintain that often a company's slogan encapsulates its culture, for example 'We try harder' or 'The appliance of science'. In a cacophonous world of corporate advertising, public relations and media hype, we can never be short of examples. Deal and Kennedy maintain that successful companies have strong identities and cultures and that the paramount beliefs in the company are shared by all: all partake in the company goal and all firmly believe in the company's mission in the marketplace.

A 'strong' culture is an asset, and means are developed to pass it on from generation to generation and up and down the hierarchy. So how is it achieved? It is achieved by a set of shared values, by unique rites and rituals and by the operation of the cultural network. Let us deal with these three elements in turn. Talk to half a dozen people in a strong culture company and pretty soon the dominant value system emerges. For instance, there can be a warm respect for the ingenuity and labour of the founder, or there can be the feeling that past 'stars' in the organisation have been right or wrong in a momentous way or (best of all) that all personnel are personally responsible for the ultimate destiny of the company. Rites and rituals are strong too: perhaps the most commonly-encountered 'rite' for the young graduate is the well known 'hazing rite'. Here the earnest young graduate high flyer, all hot with enthusiasm and ambition and fresh from college is systematically 'brought down a peg or two'. How is it done? By giving them impossible or silly tasks to do. Tasks that are excruciatingly humdrum, impossibly tough or just plain silly. It is the technological equivalent of sending the 'green' apprentice or novice off to look for a left-handed screwdriver.

In strong company cultures the cultural network is populated by characters who are instantly recognisable. For instance there are the storytellers or those people who are a direct influence on the way we see the company. They are garrulous and are fond of recalling parables and stories that serve as an example to motivate others. The story of how the marketing delegation brought the company back from insolvency; the story of how the boss staked everything on one last-ditch risk venture; the story of how the computer staff worked nights, weekends and holidays to save the company's data. In like manner the company will have its 'priests' too. These folk, usually older and wiser, see themselves as the guardians of the company's real historical values. They will often, like pontificating priests or near-senile judges, be reactionary and stick ruthlessly to old outdated creeds: 'In the old days, before we were bought out, things were better'.

'Gossips' flit about the organisation like town criers or like troubadours of old, spreading the news and the gossip. Their tit-bits of information, gleaned from every source, are always listened to; they may be trivial tittle-tattle but nevertheless we all lend them our ears. Why? Simply because the trivial gossip just might have monumental consequences. Especially if it is salacious. 'Gossips' usually precede their little stories with statements like, 'Now don't tell anyone I told you this'. Or alternatively, 'This is supposed to be absolutely hush-hush'. This unfailingly ensures it's spread like wildfire.

The four dominant types of culture are the tough-guy/macho culture, the work hard/play hard culture, the bet your company culture and process culture. These four are however ideal types and rarely exist in a 'pure' form; usually instead we find a subtle mixture or overlay of two or even more. Departments or units within an organisation may differ. A brief overview is given in figures 5.2, 5.3 and 5.4. The tough guy/macho is perfectly exemplified by the multimillionaire media moguls. These transnational corporations spanning TV, satellites, publishing and printing are undoubtedly gruelling cultures to work for. In them there is little reward to be had by cooperative work styles; instead toughness, maintaining a front, attempting to become a unique star in the system are the norm. Not surprisingly, women working in classic macho cultures such as entertainment, brewing, building or management consultancy often report blocked careers: they can rise so far and no further. Despite ambition, grit and determination, despite running twice as hard as their male counterparts, they are defeated by the combination of overt and covert sexism and a macho culture. Not for them the upper echelons of corporate power.

A work hard/play hard culture is characterised by people undertaking a high level of rather low risk activity. Success comes with dogged persistence; the risk of cataclysmic crashes is low since there are so many checks and balances within the system. A frequent downfall of this type of culture occurs when a 'quick-fix' solution is chosen when the business is in trouble. Examples of this type of culture are typically (though not always) found in computer companies, fast food chains and estate agency work. For a hugely entertaining, if somewhat partisan, account of the 'quick-fix' culture created by Sir Clive Sinclair in the UK in his various ventures see Adamson and Kennedy (1986). The culture of Acorn Computers as well as other computer manufacturers is described by Lloyd (1984).

A high risk but slow feedback environment is found in capital goods companies and in oil, car manufacturing and aviation. These are termed 'bet your company' cultures. An overall sense of making the right decision communicates itself right the way through the organisation, and

CULTURE TYPE	DESCRIPTION	EXAMPLES	SURVIVORS/HEROES	RITUALS
TOUGH GUY/MACHO	HIGH RISK QUICK FEEDBACK	CONSTRUCTION ADVERTISING COSMETICS TELEVISION ENTERTAINMENT BREWING	MAKE QUICK DECISIONS ACCEPT RISKS INDIVIDUALISTS AIM TO BECOME STARS OVERNIGHT	RELY ON CHANCE DEVISE RITUALS TO PROTECT THEMSELVES ALLOW PEOPLE TO BELIEVE THEY CAN DO WHAT THEY ARE SUPPOSED TO
WORK HARD PLAY HARD	LOW RISK QUICK FEEDBACK	ESTATE AGENCIES COMPUTER COMPANIES DOOR TO DOOR SALES FAST FOOD CHAINS	SUPER SALES PEOPLE	CONTESTS MEETINGS PROMOTIONS CONFERENCES
BET YOUR COMPANY	HIGH RISK SLOW FEEDBACK	CAPITAL GOODS MINING OIL COMPANIES	A LOT OF CHARACTER & CONFIDENCE SELF-DIRECTED, TOUGH, HAVE STAMINA TO SURVIVE WAITING PERIOD	THE BUSINESS MEETING
PROCESS	LOW RISK SLOW FEEDBACK, IF ANY	GOVERNMENT BANKS INSURANCE COMPANIES INDUSTRIES WITH CLOSE GOVERNMENT REGULATION. E.G. PHARMACEUTICALS	ORDERLY, PUNCTUAL ATTEND TO DETAIL SURVIVE ON PROTECTING SYSTEMS INTEGRITY	CENTRE OF WORK PATTERNS/LONG MEETINGS TIGHTLY STRUCTURED HIERARCHY. THE RITUAL OF REORGANISATION

Fig. 5.2. Organisation Culture.

CULTURE TYPE	STRENGTHS/ WEAKNESSES	DRESS	HOUSING	SPORTS
MACHO	QUICK FEEDBACK BUT DIVERTS RESOURCES FROM LONG TERM INVESTMENT	IN FASHION DIFFERENT FROM PEERS	'IN PLACE' ALSO HAVE VACATION HOME	ONE TO ONE e.g. TENNIS SQUASH RELY ON KILLER INSTINCT
WORK HARD PLAY HARD	HIGH VOLUME OF OUTPUT BUT QUALITY MIGHT SUFFER. LACK OF THOUGHTFULNESS. IF IN TROUBLE GO FOR QUICK FIX SOLUTION	AVOID EXTREMES STAY WITH THE NORM	PROUD OF HOUSE STAY IN SAME HOUSE FOR 20 YEARS	TEAM SPORTS THAT REQUIRE A LOT OF ACTION e.g. FOOTBALL
BET YOUR COMPANY	LEAD TO HIGH QUALITY INVENTIONS BUT SLOWLY. VULNERABLE TO SHORT TERM FLUCTUATIONS IN ECONOMY. CASH FLOW PROBLEM WHILE WAITING FOR VENTURE TO PAY OFF	CONSERVATIVE TENDS TO COINCIDE WITH THEIR RANK	LIVE IN SUBURBS RELATIVELY FAR OUT OF TOWN TUDOR DESIGN	GOLF - GOOD GAME DON'T KNOW WHETHER YOU'VE WON UNTIL 18TH HOLE
PROCESS	PUT ORDER INTO WORK THAT NEEDS TO BE PREDICTABLE. FULL OF 'RED TAPE'	AS ABOVE	FLATS OR SIMPLE 'NO FRILLS' HOMES SUBURBS CLOSE TO WORK	JOGGING SWIMMING WALKING

Fig. 5.3. Organisation Culture (contd).

CULTURE TYPE	LANGUAGE	GREETING RITUALS	CO-WORKER RITUALS
MACHO	USE WORDS NO ONE HAS EVER HEARD OF TAKE COMMON WORDS MAKE THEM UNCOMMON	RECEPTIONIST HARDLY PAYS ATTENTION TO YOU HAVE TO WAIT A MINIMUM OF 20 MINS	SCORE POINTS OFF ONE ANOTHER
WORK HARD/ PLAY HARD	USE ACRONYMS SPORTS METAPHORS	MEET YOU AT THE DOOR TAKE YOUR COAT, CUP OF COFFEE WAITING	DRINK TOGETHER
BET YOUR COMPANY	CONSTANTLY REFERRING TO HISTORY	EXPECT TO MEET ONE PERSON BUT ACTUALLY MEET FIVE	MENTOR EACH OTHER
PROCESS	ANSWER ANY QUESTION WITH A DETAILED EXPLANATION. LIKE ASKING THE SPECIFIC QUESTION THAT NO ONE CAN ANSWER	BOTH YOU AND YOUR APPOINTMENT WILL RELATE TO EACH OTHER THROUGH PAPER	DISCUSS MEMOS

Fig. 5.4. Organisation Culture (contd).

for that reason 'many heads are better than one' becomes the operative phrase. The business meeting thus assumes paramount importance. Because waiting periods between new ideas and the eventual pay-off are so long, the heroes of this type of company need tremendous strength of will and a great deal of charisma. De Lorean, the erstwhile car manufacturer, was for a time the archetypal architect of such a culture.

The process culture is found in organisations which are bureaucratic. The banking, insurance and finance sectors as well as government departments fit the description here. People concentrate on how the work is done and often receive little or no feedback on how they are doing. The overriding work ethic is to make sure that your performance at work is as technically perfect as possible, and that your faults (if you admit to them) are well covered up. Elaborate status hierarchies make for a rather formal atmosphere of deference and protocol. Thus it is all the more critical that information technology decisions, when taken at the strategic level, are seen to be the correct ones. This issue is explored more fully in the following chapter.

Strong culture companies take all of their rituals deadly seriously and since a link exists between strength and dominance of a company's culture and its success it is not surprising that a 'culture building' industry has developed. For a fee (usually huge) consultants will attempt culture building programmes for a company. In some respects though a company's culture can be more powerful than its management. Here culture can control the manager rather more than the manager can control the culture.

5.12 ORGANISATIONAL CHANGE AND WORK ROLE TRANSITIONS

People sell their labour in a labour market which is vastly different from 20, even 10 years ago. It is often said, sadly, that company 'loyalty' is a thing of the past. Few employees see the company as anything more than just an instrument from which to gain material betterment. If the pay and prospects seem better elsewhere, then they are immediately off. Promises of jam tomorrow and sticking with the company through lean times just do not seem to wash with today's employees. In yuppie culture the cash nexus rules. This may almost sound as though there was at one time a golden age when loyalty and long unquestioning devoted service were the norm; that people were in those days unmoved by material betterment. Length of stay in jobs has considerably shortened over the years, and the frequency with which people experience work role transitions has increased. It is almost a byproduct of computerisation that organisational change will take place, and organisations in a state of flux now seem to be the rule rather than the exception. Indeed, for certain types of organisation (process cultures) the reorganisation itself becomes a major cultural ritual and ceremony.

In one of the few serious studies undertaken on the phenomenon of work role transitions in modern organisational life Nicholson (1986) notes that the rate of transition is increasing. Most people today can expect a major work transition on average once every three years. For younger managers in the fast-moving organisation it can be as low as once every nine months. Of course it can be company policy to be in a constant state of flux and there is a sense in which the high speed of organisational change and resultant work role transitions can have a sort of 'gyroscope effect'. A company can achieve organisational stability through a continuous flurry of movement.

The effects of turbulence on management and staff efficiency in technology-led businesses seem poorly documented. It is an area companies would obviously prefer to ignore rather than fund research into. There is one organisation, a heavy user of information technology, which has however been examined: the US Army. Gabriel (1985), an ex US army general, attributes the poor fighting track record of the army – the long catalogue of failure in skirmishes from Grenada to Tehran – basically to rotational turbulence or the disruption caused to the system by both work role transitions and rapid personnel turnover. He states that in 1980 81% of the Army's officers and enlisted personnel changed assignment rotation and he goes on to state categorically that 'Most American units turn over once every three months'. When it comes to Air Force maintenance personnel, 84% have had less then three years' experience on equipment. Gabriel's prognosis for the US Army's success in future escapades, given this degree of turbulence, is either alarming or comforting depending upon your perception of the US Army as either naked aggressor or aggrieved peacekeeper. 'If the Army is forced to battle, it will most likely be unable to sustain itself as a combat force of any size for very long, perhaps only ten days.'

Turbulence in the organisation undergoing technology-led change is worst at the two extremes. Rapid expansion and the growth of business volume cause a crisis in staff familiarisation and training. Business direction and identity can be easily lost as people lose their way in times of change. Likewise stagnation and falling business volumes soon start people voting with their feet and taking their labour elsewhere.

5.13 CONCLUSION

The management of technology-led change need not be a hit-or-miss affair. The conclusions as to the best way to manage lie written in the empirical studies; it is up to management educators and communicators to bring these out into working practice. A prime objective must be to make management self-aware – aware of the unquestioned assumptions it possesses about people and technology, and other unquestioned assumptions it has about the implementation process. People resist change and they do so for a number of reasons. Smart management counters resistance even before it can gain momentum. It does this not by cloak and dagger policies designed to pull the wool over the eyes of employees, but instead by enlightened, open, participatory policies. Finally, management itself is a product of an organisation's culture. Knowing when the culture is becoming repressive and resistant to change requires first-class analytic thought at the highest strategic levels. The next chapter addresses these and other related issues.

5.14 REFERENCES

Adamson I. & Kennedy R. (1986) *Sinclair and the 'Sunrise' Technologies: The Deconstruction of a Myth.* Penguin, London.
Benbaset I. & Taylor R.N. (1978) The impact of cognitive styles on information system design. *MIS Quarterly*, June, 43–54.
Cornuelle R. (1975) *De-Managing America: The Final Revolution.* Randon House, New York.
Deal T.E. & Kennedy A.E. (1982) *Corporate Cultures: The Rites and Rituals of Corporate Life.* Addison Wesley, London.
Drucker P.F. (1970) *Technology Management and Society.* Heinemann, London.
Drucker P.F. (1980) *Managing in Turbulent Times.* Heinemann, London.
Gabriel R.A. (1985) *Military Incompetence: Why the American Military Doesn't Win.* Hill and Wang, New York.
Hirscheim R. & Newman M. (1988) Information systems and user resistance theory and practice. *The Computer Journal*, **31**(5), 398–408.

Institute of Management Studies (1988) *Information Technology and Managers: Some Good Practice*. Institute of Manpower Studies, University of Sussex.

Kearney A.T. (1985) *The Barriers and Opportunities of Information Technology: A Management Perspective*. Institute of Administrative Management and the Department of Trade and Industry, London.

Kling R. & Iacona S. (1984) The control of information systems development after implementation. *Communications of the Association for Computing Machinery*, **27**(12), 1218–26.

Kobler Unit (1988) *Does Information Technology Slow You Down?* Kobler Unit for the Management of Information Technology, Imperial College, University of London.

Lansdale M. (1988) The psychology of personal information management. *Applied Ergonomics*, **19**(1), 55–66.

Lloyd T. (1984) *Dinosaur and Company*. Kegan Paul, London.

Martin C.J. (1988) *Computers and Senior Managers: Top Management's Response to Interactive Computing*. National Computer Centre, Manchester.

Nicholson N. (1986) Turning points, traps and tunnels: the significance of work role transitions in the lives of individuals and organisations. In *The Psychology of Work and Organisations* (Ed. by G. Debus & H.W. Schroiff). North Holland Elsevier Science.

Robey D. (1983) Information systems and organisational change: a comparative case study. *Systems, Objectives, Solutions*, **3**, 143–54.

Steiner G. (1975) *After Babel: Aspects of Language and Translation*. Oxford University Press, Oxford.

Steiner G. (1978) *On Difficulty*. Oxford University Press, Oxford.

Tapscott D. *et al.* (1987) *Planning for Implementing Office Systems*. Dow Jones Irwin, Homewood, Illinois.

Yaverbaum G.T. & Sherr D.M. (1986) Experimental results towards the customizing of information systems. *Human Relations*, **39**(2), 117–34.

Chapter 6
Conclusion: strategy and organisations of the future

6.1 OVERVIEW

This final chapter looks at the strategic decisions all organisations have to make about information technology. They will need to ask questions like 'What is the importance of information technology to our survival?' 'How can we best use it?' 'Where will it lead us?'. The chapter classifies businesses into sectors depending on the centrality of information technology to their survival, and we look at the thinking and models which drive businesses forward in these various sectors. The chapter continues by examining the practical ways organisations can begin to evaluate the total worth of information technology. Finally, because of the speed with which organisations can change and adapt to changing world circumstances, an agenda for ecological responsibility for future organisations is advanced.

6.2 DO BUSINESSES HAVE INFORMATION TECHNOLOGY STRATEGIES?

A business, no matter how large or small, will only have a strategy for information technology if it represents a substantial part of its budget. So the first question to ask is how much do businesses actually spend on information technology? Obviously this depends on which sector we are talking about because clearly banking and insurance invest much more heavily than does, say, the building sector. We can only speak in ratio terms since absolute amounts are meaningless and, what is more, when ratios are mentioned by professional economists more than a pinch of salt is needed. Price Waterhouse (1988) claim that the 'average' UK business spends 0.97% of sales revenue on information technology, although finance and leisure businesses may be nearer 5.1%. Various figures are bandied about periodically by other public and private agencies and considerable debate (as usual) surrounds the estimates; but what is beyond doubt is that total spending is colossal: despite economic ups and downs it is a multimillion pound industry, growing exponentially in certain areas.

Most, if not all, large organisations have had information technology strategies in operation for a number of years. By this we mean that they have a discrete set of executive decisions to be made about if, when, where, how and why to deploy information technology. For these organisations it has been an item near the top of the chairman's agenda for a number of years, talked about and argued over and always never far from the limelight. For medium to small firms, one study (Galliers 1988) found that 84% of UK companies were formulating information technology or information systems plans of a strategic or long-term nature. Since it appears there is so much of this activity going on, the process of strategy formulation deserves our critical scrutiny.

6.3 A SECTOR FRAMEWORK FOR INFORMATION TECHNOLOGY

In chapter 1 it was suggested that the best possible classification for understanding the impact of information technology on people and organisations was the one based upon what it actually did. The five-fold classification based upon function was then used. In this chapter a classification will be adopted which is based upon the value of information technology to the organisation's survival, together with the attributes of the technology itself. This sector framework, developed by Earl (1989), has the advantage of using a classification system already present to a large extent in everyday speech. It is therefore readily understood.

First there is a sector of business which is absolutely dependent on information technology for its survival. Technology is the very means of 'delivering the goods', hence it is appropriately labelled the 'delivery' sector. Often computer-based transaction systems hold the whole business outfit together. Financial services, commodities trading, the futures market, airlines, tour operators and increasingly retailing all fall into this category. What happens to business in this sector? Customers will flock to the better services or goods on offer made possible by the latest state-of-the-art technology. Fall behind in the race to incorporate and exploit the latest gadget and you could be bounced right out of the race altogether.

Second, there is the sector of business that is becoming increasingly dependent on information technology for survival. This sector is labelled the 'dependent' sector. To survive and expand the businesses increasingly need to automate or install computer-based systems of one sort or another. Examples are found in car manufacturing and textiles (CAM or computer aided manufacture and CAD or computer aided design) and the spares supply industry.

The third sector is one that sees information technology as perhaps only potentially capable of providing new strategic opportunities and business drive. This is therefore labelled the 'drive' sector. Continuous process and food manufacturing industries are examples.

Last, the sector referred to as 'delayed' is one that technology has had, as yet, no strategic impact on. 'Yet' is the operative word, for although the opportunities or threats from computerisation are not yet apparent, they might well be so in the future. Most of remaining business and industry could well be located here.

So where does a sectorial analysis get us? It should set us thinking hard about how a company can make a conscious, strategic decision to migrate across classifications. How, for instance, does a company hoist itself up the ladder, how does it change from being in a delayed position (and hence extremely vulnerable) to being, say, dependent? Building societies give instructive examples here. Within the space of two or three years they have moved from being simply mortgage processors to providing a whole range of financial services: home banking, portfolio management, insurance, legal assistance with house purchase and so on. It was a strategic opportunity given to the business 'on a plate' by the phenomenally rapid development of hardware and software in the field. Industry strategists actively exploited deregulation to the full, with a degree of success visible for all to see.

What characterises the thinking of the top strategists and decision-makers in each of the four types? We find that each is operating with a clearly defined strategic model. For industries in the delivery sector we find that thinking is definitely systems and technology orientated. Bankers have to be acutely aware of developments on the horizon in automatic teller machine technology and remote banking via the customer's domestic telephone linked to the bank's mainframe. It is in this very real sense that we say that the delivery sector is infrastructure-led; with the paradigm case of banking more or less dependent on hardware and software architecture developments. However, although capital investment in systems is huge and on-going, banks are keen never to lose sight of human needs. It might well be that the public might not be ready to accept certain impersonal automated facilities or the complete absence of the high street bank.

Thinking in the dependent sector is somewhat different. Strategists will be continually looking over their shoulders with an eye on what their competitors are doing. For example, in engineering fabrication it is known that computer-controlled machine tools can cut costs and be a potent facilitator of company growth. At the present time at least, for large swathes of engineering, firms are more interested in information systems – computerised stock control, accounting software, purchasing and invoicing – than in computer-aided manufacture. If the management information system can first be sorted out and rationalised it can form the basis for future high-cost investment in the newer generation of machine tools.

One manufacturing chairman illustrates this 'looking over the shoulder' mentality perfectly. His product uses metal-bending technology – traditionally slower to computerise than metal-forming (milling, grinding, shaping) technology. One direct competitor had recently installed a (significantly, German) computer-controlled metal-bending machine. After an invited visit to view the set-up, the chairman said

> 'It seems to me the technology is as yet far too unreliable. It (the machine) is only operating at below 50% capacity with lots of teething troubles yet to be sorted out. Of course the settling-in process will be catered for in the purchase contract, but as yet I am not sure the high capital outlay costs can be justified in terms of labour cost savings. Unit costs will remain high. At the plant they have got three men trying full time to get it up and running. It might be premature to judge but I think that their labour costs are high if not higher than in our plant! I shall keep my ear to the ground and review the situation in six months' time'.

Thinking in the 'drive' sector will be towards less obvious strategic gains. Here people are opportunity-led or seduced by product hype, rather than by a careful analysis of the market. The main stumbling block is the massive cost of investment in information technology for which no glaring strategic gain can be seen. They are just not convinced, likewise firms in the 'delayed' sector.

6.4 INFORMATION TECHNOLOGY AND COMPETITION: THE RESPONSES OF FIRMS

When a firm first begins to assemble a strategic plan for information technology it needs to articulate fully the nature of the competitive forces acting upon it. Now if we were simply to sit down and list all the competitive forces acting upon a firm, to classify and assemble them into coherent labels, we would end up with just five. This is what the seminal work of Porter (1980) is best known for. His book *Competitive Strategy* has established itself as something of an industry standard for the strategic planner. In it he states that for strategic planning purposes five competitive forces can be labelled. First there is the threat of new entrants to the same market, threatening to grab market share, put you out of business. Second there is the dangerous bargaining power suppliers have over you ('costs will have to go up by 30% unless you start to order in bulk from us on a regular basis'). Third there is the bargaining power of customers ('I am a regular customer, can I have trade terms now please?'). Fourth there is the threat of substitute products or services ('Our product undersells yours by 15%'). Finally all competitive forces result in the fact that the firm will be jostling for position among rivals ('We are losing our market share to X company, our traditional rivals in the marketplace').

Information technology has quite specific effects on strategy in each of these competitive areas. Most dynamically and excitingly, information technology can be used for 'leverage' of a business. By this is meant the ability to jack up market share, to up the business profile, to increase profits directly and dramatically. In a series of *Harvard Business Review* articles McFarlan (1984), Cash and Konsynski (1985) and Porter and Millar (1985) analysed how it is done. Let us take the forces in turn. How can a firm use information technology to stop new entrants from grabbing their market share? What specifically can technology do here? The first and most obvious thing it can do is help erect direct barriers to entry for the interlopers. For established, wealthy businesses this means investing heavily in technology, purchasing better state-of-the-art hardware and using chips in products. It all adds up to the same thing: the stakes are raised, often prohibitively, against the newcomer.

The case example I wish to cite here is one relating to my own business experience. I designed, manufactured and marketed a skin galvanometer. This is a simple biofeedback device revealing the state of physiological arousal by measuring the electrical conductivity in the skin. Tight costs dictated a 'low tech' printed circuit board (PCB) mounted transistorised amplifier. The innovation came in the self-instruction material supplied with the machine – in this case booklets and audio tapes explaining the use of the instrument for a variety of serious and not-so-serious activities (stress management, arousal games with partners, party games and lying games – for the skin galvanometer had at that time gained some notoriety as an alleged 'lie detector'). Marketing was mainly through mail order advertising in selected publications (Winfield and Winfield 1985).

An established manufacturer 'upped the stakes' by bringing out an instrument based upon microprocessor technology. Miniaturisation allowed the instrument to be reduced in size to a hand-held card giving a digital read out instead of a costly analogue swing galvanometer. Wires and cumbersome electrodes were likewise superseded. In all, vastly improved portability and robustness gave it instant mass market appeal. Marketed via a nationally-known marketing outfit it effectively pushed small fish entrants like myself painfully out into the cold. Of course there was nothing to stop entrants embarking on costly new product developments based on chip technology but the stakes were too high for the small time punter: the risks were too high.

How can information technology manage the relationship with the supplier better? To a certain extent this has been dealt with already in chapter 1, for we can easily see that we can scan suppliers' prices and performances if we have an up-to-date database. Developments in interorganisational systems, information brokerage and electronic document interchange will all permit easy on-line scanning or periodic analyses of the best delivery schedule. All of these strategies let information technology reduce the power suppliers have.

Customers exert their own particular brand of tyranny over business. Information technology can easily 'lock them in' to a particular company, for example in the following way. It can easily make the costs of switching a disincentive: in this respect witness the myriad and costly charges slapped on when a customer changes banks. Another strategy would be to let information technology inform the business better about the buying behaviour and other characteristics of the customer. A more careful analysis of needs and wants would allow more careful target marketing of the firm's other products (including new ones). We know already that technology can change the very basis of competition and the jockeying for position among rivals. It can change the name of the game, as observed already in the change in the nature of business in both banking and building societies.

6.5 EVALUATING INFORMATION TECHNOLOGY

To the businessman it is always the bottom line which talks loudest. Is it worth it? Does it contribute to increased profit? Could I sell all the expensive gadgetry and still make a handsome profit? Have we been ripped off mercilessly by computer salesman hype? Evaluation might seem a fairly cut and dried affair, after all it seems a simple activity to record bottom line profits first before and then after computerisation. In reality it is not so simple a procedure. Businesses are continually changing their markets and they might well be operating in a world vastly different today, when computerisation is complete, from what it was say three years ago. Compounding the issue is the fact that accounting practices differ – for some firms information technology is an expense and for others it is an investment. This variability in practice leads Earl (1989) to note, somewhat sardonically, 'In the author's experience, the accounting treatment of information technology is varied, ad hoc, often arbitrary and sometimes absent'. Better still is his terse conclusion: 'The benefits of some information technology projects are so immense in productivity, leverage or business development terms that net present value, accounting rate of return or payback calculations become outrageous and incongruous'.

Leaving aside the bickerings of accountants (for the interested reader, well summarised in McKerrow 1988), a behaviourally based and practical approach to evaluation is given by Clegg *et al.* (1988). The authors claim from their studies of firms' practices that successful evaluation is based on seven propositions. Let us examine these in turn. The first proposition states that evaluation should concentrate on the tasks to be done, not merely the computerised system. All too often evaluation is targetted at a particular piece of hardware: the target should be the whole department or company, for the hardware is in existence merely to support their objectives. This proposition refers to the kind of tunnel vision associated with narrow efficiency criteria. Increased effectiveness should be the goal.

The second proposition states that evaluation should be orientated towards action. Since the objective is improved performance the whole exercise should not be started unless one is unflinchingly prepared to change things. Next, the evaluation exercise has to be systematic, leaving aside no untested assumption. Ideally the exercise should involve only a small number of individuals working to a specified timetable. The next proposition states that the exercise should be aimed at looking beyond the obvious problems: how low operator output, for instance, might be caused by a number of interrelated factors both hardware-based and organisationally-based. The next proposition states that evaluation works best when as wide a range of staff as possible are engaged in the information gathering exercise. Participation draws upon a wide base of expertise. Interpretation and subsequent action may not be open to such democratic egalitarian measures. The sixth proposition states that evaluation should be comparative. By this the authors mean that where possible reference should be made to the performance of competitors with similar systems and/or comparisons made with established industry 'benchmarks' or published performance standards. The final proposition states that evaluation should be tailor made to meet local needs, in other words the particular contemporary objectives that the company has. In order to systematise the whole evaluation process the authors provide ready made questionnaires and checklists.

6.6 ORGANISATIONAL TRANSFORMATION AND INFORMATION TECHNOLOGY

There are a number of clear pointers to success in the strategic exploitation of information technology. If it is successful it will inevitably result in a degree of organisational transformation. We should not be afraid of the idea of change. If it takes place in the right direction, congruent with emergent business conditions and a better more whole-some environment, then change should be welcomed. But where do the ideas for transformation come from within the organisation? There might be ideas for a whole range of activities, for new business directions, for new products, for new organisational structures. All of these originate in the minds of people employed within the organisation. Earl (1989) says our thinking on the derivation and ownership of ideas for change has been for too long dominated by 'either/or' thinking. We see ideas as either 'top down' or 'bottom up'. In the former case, ideas emanate from a small coterie of corporate decision-makers. This somewhat elitist image presupposes that there is in existence a small class of people endowed by superior intellect to be able to grasp all the complex issues involved. It is the thinking behind the emergence of the corporate 'think tank'. On the other hand, the bottom up metaphor sees the mass of employees as valuable resources. The old factory suggestion box has been given a smartening up recently as organisations are drawing on ideas and values which they see more uniformly dispersed throughout the organisation.

Earl goes for an interesting third approach, an approach neither top down nor bottom up. He calls it the 'inside out' approach, whereby line management should be given their head. Studies of innovation in organisation, he claims, seem to reveal that it is line managers who so often set the ball rolling. For Earl it is the bright spark individuals, solidly in the middle of the organisation, who really count. These bold imaginative would-be entrepreneurs have to be actively encouraged and given a degree of licence.

It is an appealing, essentially Western liberal-democratic notion to think that ideas are dispersed evenly throughout the organisation and all that an organisation has to do is trawl for them in the most likely areas. Fish in the line management ranks, for it is they who have painstakingly risen from the ranks and know the workings inside out and have all the best ideas, or so the thinking goes. It is heartening to see that in times of turbulence and change many organisations are actively encouraging their 'ideas people' to assert themselves more. The effort seems to be directed at encouraging what are termed 'intrapreneurs' – folk who take the initiative, lead others to change, see opportunities where others see only barriers, and are prepared to take risks. These are qualities that organisations should nurture. Unfortunately much of the experience of young, bright people in organisations is exactly the opposite. The sad fact is that far too many organisations are overconcerned with the control element. Overconcerned with keeping people in their place, teaching them to be deferential, teaching them to wait their turn, socialising them to mind-numbing routine. Many people speak of being subjected to deadening conformist thinking. One entertaining approach uses black humour to make us think about how organisations stifle imaginative people. Kanter (1983) lists 10 rules (see below) that organisations use to quench the fires of imaginative thinking. The rules alert us to the prevalence of negative, repressive behaviour in organisations. But who among us can deny, hand on heart, ever having used some of these tactics at some time?

(1) Regard any new ideas coming up from below with suspicion. Why? Because they are both new and from below.

(2) Insist that people who need your approval to act first have to go through several other levels of management to obtain their signatures. Maximise the hassle involved.

(3) Ask departments or individuals to challenge and criticise each other's proposals. This saves you the tedious job of deciding – you just plump for the survivor.

(4) Express your criticisms freely, but always withhold your praise. This serves to keep people on their toes. Let them know periodically that they can be fired at any time.

(5) Treat identification of problems as signs of failure, so as to discourage people from letting you know when something in their area isn't working.

(6) Control everything fastidiously. Make sure people count absolutely anything that can be counted. Make sure they do this frequently.

(7) Make decisions to reorganise or change company policies in absolute secret. Always spring them on people unexpectedly and when they least expect it. (This also helps to keep people on their toes.)

(8) Make sure that requests for information are fully justified, and make sure that information is not given out to managers too freely. (You don't want data to fall into the wrong hands.)

(9) Assign to lower-level managers, in the hallowed name of delegation and participation, responsibility for figuring out how to cut back, lay off, move people around or otherwise implement threatening decisions you have personally made. Get them to do it quickly.

(10) Above all else never forget rule number 10. You, the higher-ups, already know all that is worth knowing about this business. Only mandarins can think strategically.

Personnel policies which result in the overcontrol of people, to keep them in their place, can emanate from strategic thinking; negativity and passivity can permeate people's whole beings. It can reach a point where the first reaction to a problem encountered in the workaday world is not to attempt to solve it but to pass it on. It can permeate the whole company's culture and is damaging and insidious.

Entrepreneurs have long been the subject of behavioural study (Winfield 1983) and organisations are now keen to keep and nurture these people wherever possible. Their ideas and drive are good for the company. Put more cynically, the bright spark employee quitting with innovative ideas, having inside information and invaluable contacts, is a positive danger to the company that nurtured him or her. Within a short space of time he or she could well turn into a serious competitor. If only for this self-interested reason, organisations are now keen to use strategies to retain employees who harbour entrepreneurial symptoms. The creation of an organisational climate conducive to innovation and development and receptive to bold radical business ideas is called 'intrapreneuring'. Pinchot (1985) takes a wry look at the working life of the intrapreneur (the individual who, for all intents and purposes, works and thinks like an entrepreneur yet is located within the confines of the host organisation). Pinchot comes up with the intrapreneur's 10 commandments and they serve our purposes very well in showing up the inner workings of corporate life.

(1) Come to work each day willing to be fired.
(2) Circumvent any orders aimed at stopping your dream.
(3) Do any job needed to make your project work regardless of your job description.
(4) Find people to help you.
(5) Follow your intuition about the people you choose, and work only with the best.
(6) Work underground for as long as you can – publicity triggers the corporate immune mechanism.
(7) Never bet on a race unless you are running in it.
(8) Remember it is easier to ask forgiveness than for permission.
(9) Be true to your goals, but be realistic about the ways to achieve them.
(10) Honour your sponsors.

6.7 STRATEGY AND THE ORGANISATION OF THE FUTURE

The criticism of the capitalist mode of production has in the past always been on the basis of some written creed or other. The ideology of

Marxism is based upon the writings of Marx and Lenin; radical Muslim fundamentalism is based upon the writings of the Koran. The decadence of capitalism and Western high technology consumerism as a way of life was in the past contrasted with a few role models of societies which organised themselves along alternative socialist or religious fundamentalist lines. The role models of Eastern European communism (poor though they were) have now gone. Likewise the reborn fundamentalist state did not materialise. Huge swathes of Europe are being opened up to the power of the market.

Big businesses, conglomerates and large multinationals, like it or not, are here to stay and are ever spreading their spheres of domination globally. They will never be free of criticism and public scrutiny and people's anxieties, instead of being directed at menacing superpowers, will be directed and focussed more sharply. Gone will be the undercurrent of fear amongst populations about the outbreak of an unstoppable nuclear war (Thompson 1985). Our anxieties about the diminishing earth's resources and the ever more fragile ecosystem will be directed more and more at these huge mega business units. It is they, after all, who define our needs and ruthlessly manipulate our tastes. People will therefore want to see them taking the lead: for huge market power should carry with it the concomitant of societal responsibility. Just how that responsibility is shouldered comes more in the public eye with every passing year. Money already seems to be flowing to where it is used cleanly. Ethical investment, where the company invested in is squeaky-clean, has grown to £200 million in unit trusts. The Ethical Investment Research Service (ERIS) found that more than half of the top 50 companies listed on the stock exchange have links with producers and sellers of armaments. In the top 20 only five are clear altogether: Glaxo, British Gas, ICI, Smith Kline Beecham and Marks and Spencer.

Of course this is not to deny that people at the individual level will continue to 'do their bit' towards a better, healthier and cleaner world. They will make the personal decision to change to unleaded petrol, recycle rubbish, experiment with dietary changes and so on, but public attention and criticism will be increasingly on the big units. Why? The sheer scale of their operation and their attendant consumption of resources makes them easily identifiable targets. They can be seen to be squandering resources and speeding us on our way to ecological disaster, or they can be seen instead to be taking the lead in a new, more responsible order of things. The debate is on everybody's lips; the issues discussed in the media and whenever people meet. Should McDonald's use environmentally-friendly packaging instead of ghastly polystyrene ozone-eaters? Just how fast is General Motors taking the lead in electric vehicle propulsion?

Now that threat escalation by the superpowers is reduced what will happen to the arms and weapons manufacturers? Here the link with information technology grows ominously strong. As already noted, the main impetus for information technology has traditionally come from the 'defence' industry. Put bluntly, for more deadly and more reliable weapons delivery systems. This has been a dismal thread running through this book – the need for faster, more ruthless genocide has in the past driven technical development before it. With the outbreak of peace between the superpowers are the major defence contractors – British Aerospace, GEC, Phillips, Thorn EMI, Racal – actively moving towards peaceful, socially useful product development? Evidence seems to be forthcoming that they are choosing, not a 'swords into ploughs' policy, but are favouring a marketing push to sell their products to the skirmishes in the Third World and to participants in interethnic and racist strife.

Something has to be done, and done fast. The arms race is far from over: the phenomenal power of weapons delivery systems to swallow up resources is not diminishing but actually increasing. Technologically sophisticated weapons and aircraft are altars upon which we sacrifice our futures. The East/West arms race achieved what it intended to do: the bankruptcy of communism. In the USA at least, it looks set to bankrupt the capitalist system as well. New weapons require ever more sophisticated computer-controlled systems. The American F-16 fighter of the early 1980s needed 263 000 lines of computer code. The infamous B-1 bomber needed 1.2 million lines. The latest toy under development, the advanced tactical fighter, will have 6 million lines! According to Mark Urban (1990) 'If the demand for military and civilian software continues to increase at the current rate, an American study has shown that by 2040 every man, woman and child in the United States would have to be writing software'.

Information technology has the power to bring about changes fast. Changing consumer demands can therefore be met head on; trends quickly analysed and acted upon, newly emerging markets rapidly exploited. The public knows that technology gives organisations unparalled power to change fast, and it expects nothing short of far-sighted responsibility from them. Of course large organisations have within their powers the means to spot trends and jump on the bandwagon fast, such as adopting a public 'green image'. Unfortunately many organisations will be green in appearance only. Like the wolf in sheep's clothing, hidden menaces lurk behind an apparently benign exterior. The colour green is more likely to be the green of a mercenary combat jacket. (For a review of the multinational's predatory, warlike intentions and how the language of war is now an established part of corporate vernacular see Ramsey 1987.)

A polished green image at home can often be based on Third World exploitation and the dumping of damaging products on undeveloped countries. Surplus European Community milk being shipped out to undeveloped countries is a case in point. A society in hock to the World Bank becomes locked into an inappropriate technology (freeze dried milk and bottle feeding) and hence becomes even more dependent on the 'advanced' industrial societies.

The world, because of the mobility of capital and communications, becomes a huge 'global village'. In the words of McLuhan (1964), inhabitants of the wired-in global village are in constant communication with one another. Because of huge information flows and the associated ease of global communication people will be on the look-out for abuses of power and capital. Sinister examples are never hard to find, and find them they will, for increasingly the debate will be about instances. The particular instance of business malpractice will be seen to characterise the whole organisation. Businesses will be vigilant, actively scurrying round cleaning up their act. Sometimes though, the filth and disasters that they cause cannot be swept away or sanitised by the sweet talk of public relations experts. Like the case of Union Carbide. As I write, the leak of toxic gases at Bhopal in India in 1984 has been the worst man-made disaster the world has yet experienced. The death toll has been established at between 4300 and 20 000, with 445 000 people affected. Nearly all of the victims are pathetically poor and therefore unable to buy much justice. As an example of how a large multinational company can manage to escape control, be it at local or national level, the case makes textbook reading. The sum of £115 has been agreed for any permanently disabled victim (Editorial 1990).

In terms of an organisation's strategic goals it is easy to see that at boardroom level, official or charter goals will be assembled to meet increasingly environmentally-conscious public demands. Public relations departments and services will grow fat on the increased volume of work (cynically referred to as reworking the truth). The chattering classes, the media, and through them the public, will not be hoodwinked. They will be looking at the actual operational goals. Just what is the organisation doing in reality? What about at the local level? What does the carefully sanitised green image of the multinational count for if it daily dumps toxic waste into the local watercourse? But are we not wandering off into the domain of politics and values here? At heart lies the problem of how we should judge the practice of technology.

6.8 HUMAN VALUES AND TECHNOLOGY PRACTICE

At the heart of any examination of the relationship between business, information technology and human values lie two areas of confusion. On the one hand the term 'technology' is used so widely that in practice it has come to mean anything and everything and therefore threatens to mean nothing. This state of affairs is relatively easily rectified by stating precisely what sense of the word we are currently using; we noted in an earlier chapter the idiosyncratic uses to which writers and thinkers had put the word in the past.

The second area of confusion has far more dangerous consequences, concerned as it is with the central thesis of this book. It is that technology is perceived as value-free, somehow neutral. It is seen as simply being a tool; seen as a simple means to achieve an end. As the word is currently and narrowly being used it is quite simply not the domain of human values at all. The consequence of this restriction in meaning of the term is that our talk of developments in technology becomes emasculated, automatically narrowed. Ethical values, human considerations, the genuine talk that should take place about how things could be, all these become marginalised. We are in too much of a hurry to stop and question fundamentals, we cannot pause to reflect – our competitors may catch up. The consequence is that human needs and aspirations become neutralised. Ethical considerations are shoved in at the end of conferences or relegated to an informal seminar; textbooks on information technology have sections or chapters on societal considerations of information technology tagged on at the end. To use the phrase of Herbert Marcuse (1968) the discourse becomes one-dimensional, it admits of no opposites, allows no counter arguments and no contemplation of alternatives. We rush headlong into the Brave New World of technology only to find a hollowness: we are manic consumers knowing the price of everything and the value of nothing.

So what is wrong? We can highlight the conceptual impoverishment of our use of the term 'technology' by contrasting its current usage with that of our usage of the term 'medicine'. In current use, the term medicine has ideas within its penumbra of meanings which allow discussions about different ways of choosing ends, different ways of choosing values, different ways of serving the community. It allows a discussion on the very question of ends. 'Technology' as we use it has no such facility. More is the pity then. We therefore need the concept of technology practice to be used in the same way as the concept of medical practice. From this standpoint we will see better which aspects of technology (if any) really are value-free and which are inextricably tied up with cultural values (however disguised). We should then be able to see which dominant model of humanity is being used. Technology practice should be argued about, voted on, brought under social control. For an extended discussion on this idea see Pacey (1983).

The strictly technical aspects of technology will include the range of classic 'technological fixes'. All cures brought about by developments in technology (water pollution control, analgesics, 'cancer cures' and so on), will ignore to a greater or lesser degree how or why the irritant was there in the first place. Moving from this restricted meaning of technology we can progress to the domains which are full of attributed human values. In this domain of technological practice we have both cultural and organisational values. This suggests there should be imperatives to technology that go beyond narrow utilitarian goals. I want to advocate therefore a broadening of the meaning of the word.

Unfortunately, in the popular mind ethics and human values are seen as essentially clouding the issue, as getting in the way of advances in technology. In the frenzied atmosphere of the debate the discussion becomes denuded of all normative values. The issues become expressed with the simple slogan of the tabloid headline 'automate or liquidate'. This dominant ethos has already put an end to much research into evaluation of the impact of technology on working life. For example, the momentum of the much lauded Quality of Working Life research of the late 1970s and early 1980s has now been quashed. The results were seen as being at odds with both economy and work efficiency. You were nothing short of being a wimp if you prattled on at work about job satisfaction and personal development.

In similar vein the popular imagination (and much current management ideology too) sees as fundamentally antagonistic the twin thrusts of participation and efficiency. Thus resistance to technological advances at the workplace is perceived as delinquent, even Luddite in character. Mumford (1967) in *The Myth of the Machine* reminds us of the human traditions of our science and technology. It is an 'earth-centered', organic and human model to which civilisation must return if it is to avoid the disastrous consequences of the mega machine. Quoting from the book: 'Mankind will need to undergo something like a spontaneous religious conversion, one that will replace the mechanical world picture to give to the human personality as the highest manifestation of life the precedence it now gives to machines and computers'. That was written in 1967, computer dominance of thought and recreation is light years ahead now. In the same manner let us consider Galbraith (1972) in *The New Industrial State*: 'A society propelled by imperatives of technology is increasingly closed, inertial, inflexible, and isolated from any true conception of human needs'.

Are such sentiments to be marginalised in our culture? Are they to be relegated to the dustbin of ideas perhaps along with the antitechnologists and doomwatchers? Or are they to be tolerated merely as something quaint, perhaps the last gasp of English Liberalism? The central thesis of this book is that they should not be. Human needs and expectations become ever more bewildering in their variety and complexity as we enter the fifth generation and beyond.

6.9 CONCLUSION

All books have but a few coded messages running through them: at the end of the day they can be usually summarised in two or three motifs. This book is no exception. To become too wrapped up in and seduced by the 'wonders' of technology will lead us to neglect the all-important human element in the equation. With every advance in information technology our dependence on humans increases, not decreases. We ignore human needs at our peril.

The other theme is the prevalence of change and the magnetic attraction of the new: rush headlong and buy the best, most expensive, most powerful, state-of-the-art, top-of-the-line computerised gadget. Now more than ever before messages about new products all seem to be geared to making us dissatisfied with existing products. People's identities are made by what they purchase. Well-being is increasingly seen to be directly equated with our possessions; our self-esteem directly correlated with how quickly we can turn over our possessions. The message is clear: throw out the old, use plastic to buy in the new.

The quickening of the pace of consumer society can be attributed to the chip, for intensified commodity circulation is increasingly computer-driven. A fundamental distinction has been made by Leiss (1978) between our needs and wants. Needs are an objective state, measured, felt, real. In the same way that we need food and oxygen. Wants are more subjective, more easily manipulated by advertising. We are steeped in a religion of economic growth and individuals, in East Europe as well as West Europe, now interpret their well-being in terms of the degree of success they have in turning over their possessions as dictated by fashion. What characterises phoney wants in the market-intensive society we now live in? According to Leiss we are engaged in a headlong pursuit without stopping to do the one thing that we can do better than any computer, chip, neural network or supercomputer. It is simply to sit and reflect. Where are we heading? Where is the market-intense life we lead taking us? No computer will ever throw up on screen such fundamental questions.

Politicians have always grovelled to jump on bandwagons. And the bandwagon of white-hot progress through technical success has been a favourite for decades. In this sense the future has been highjacked by computers. Anything they touch, Midas-like, turns to gold. Yet we somehow know that that which we seem to desire so urgently today will be forgotten, almost despised, tomorrow. Today's gadget will be rapidly superseded by tomorrow's better, more expensive gadget. According to Leiss:

'The accelerating rate of product turnover provides a clue to the shallowness of wants in the prevailing market setting: things that appear so indispensable one day, only to be discarded in favour of others the next, cannot be presumed to stir the wellsprings of desire very deeply.'

Time to pause, to reflect on where technology is taking us is thus called for. Manic pursuit of progress, technical perfection without purpose and ever-expanding business may just stop us asking ourselves fundamental questions. But then humans are good at avoiding such things are they not? As we have seen, a theme of this book has been the degree to which computers force us into a state of self-deception. Throw money away, be seduced by promises of greater efficiency, yet see net gains of zero at the end of the day. The avoidance of fundamental questions in the market-driven society perhaps explains the increased interest in religion and mysticism in all post industrial societies.

Organisations are fundamentally about social modes of existence, and both organisations and society are being transformed by computer technology. To ask whether society and organisations are making modern life spiritually satisfying is to beg certain questions. Questions such as whether spiritually satisfying means living in accordance with some religious creed? Alternatively one can adopt a humanist stance and ask whether computer technology culture is life-enhancing? Does it contribute to the sum joy of human life? Are we enriched, more in tune with one another, are we interacting with grace and mutual consideration? Or do we see ourselves in a perpetual state of deprivation, of needing more, of consuming more yet left feeling more harassed, more deprived? In evaluating the kind of life our organisations and dominant computer culture are foisting upon us I wish to use the term 'conviviality', as used in a particularly enlightening way by Illich (1973):

'Far from being the state of tipsy inebriation it has come to mean in popular usage in fact it possesses connotations of co-operative interaction all too absent in computer driven societies. I choose the term 'conviviality' to describe the opposite of industrial productivity. I intend it to mean autonomous and creative intercourse among persons, and the intercourse of persons with their environment ... I consider conviviality to be individual freedom realised in personal interdependance and, as such, an intrinsic ethical value. I believe that, in any society, as conviviality is reduced below a certain level, no amount of industrial productivity can effectively satisfy the need it creates among society's members.'

There are advanced industrial societies on the face of this globe where the quality of life is nothing short of ghastly. Civility, pleasure in social intercourse for its own sake, the graceful enjoyment of beauty – all seem completely gone. The people are hell bent on making money, on developing the next generation chip. They are societies steadily ageing into selfishness, for children are too expensive: they get in the way of the pursuit of the latest material gizmo.

At the end of the day what images and memories do we take with us as we go gently into that dark night? We don't for sure remember our objects, our gadgets, our cars, our computers. We remember the fundamentals, things forever beyond the power of money to buy: the warmth of human love, the indescribable joy in the voice of a child's song.

6.10 REFERENCES

Cash J.I. & Konsynski B.R. (1985) I.S. redraws the competitive boundaries. *Harvard Business Review*, March–April.

Clegg C. *et al.* (1988) *People and Computers: How to Evaluate your Company's New Technology*. Ellis Horwood, Chichester.

Earl M.J. (1989) *Management Strategies for Information Technology*. Prentice-Hall, London.

Editorial (1990) *New Statesman and Society*, 26 January.

Galbraith J.K. (1972) *The New Industrial State*. Deutsch, London.

Galliers R. (1988) I.T. strategies today: the U.K. experience. In *Information Management: The Strategic Dimension* (Ed. by M.J. Earl). Oxford University Press, Oxford.

Illich I.D. (1973) *Tools for Conviviality*. Marion Boyars, London.

Kanter R.M. (1983) *The Change Masters*. Allen and Unwin, London.

Leiss W. (1978) *The Limits to Satisfaction*. Marion Boyars, London.

Lindblom A. (1959) The science of muddling through. *Public Administration Review*.

McFarlan F.W. (1984) Information technology changes the way you compete. *Harvard Business Review*, May–June.

McKerrow P. (1988) *Performance Measurement of Computer Systems*. Addison Wesley, London.

McLuhan M. (1964) *Understanding Media*. Routledge and Kegan Paul, London.

Marcuse H. (1968) *One Dimensional Man*. Routledge, London.

Mumford E. (1967) *The Myth of the Machine*. Secker and Warberg, London.

Pacey H. (1983) *The Culture of Technology*. Blackwell, Oxford.

Pinchot G. (1985) *Intrapreneuring*. Harper and Row, London.

Porter M.E. (1980) *Competitive Strategy*. Free Press, New York.

Porter M.E. & Millar V.E. (1985) How information gives you competitive advantage. *Harvard Business Review*, July–August.

Price Waterhouse (1988) *Information Technology Review 1987/88*. Price Waterhouse, London.

Ramsey D.K. (1987) *The Corporate Warriors: The Battle of the Boardroom*. Grafton, London.

Simon H.A. (1949) *Administrative Behaviour*. Free Press, New York.

Thompson D. (1985) *Psychological Aspects of Nuclear War*. The British

Psychological Society and Wiley, Chichester.

Urban M. (1990) Navy discovers high cost of computerised aircraft. *The Independant*, 29 January.

Winfield I.J. (1983) *People in Business*. Heinemann, London.

Winfield I.J. & Winfield A.E. (1985) Designing and manufacturing an educational technology product. In *Aspects of Educational Technology XVIII: New Directions in Education and Training Technology* (Ed. by B.S. Alloway and G.M. Mills). Kogan Page, London.

Index